Donald Judd

Cover: View of concrete works
Chinati Foundation, Marfa, Texas

Frontispiece A: Installation of concrete
work, Chinati Foundation, Marfa, Texas

Frontispiece B: *Untitled*, 1984
Concrete and steel, three units: 98$7/16$ x
98$7/16$ x 98$7/16$ in. (250 x 250 x 250 cm) each
Collection of Laumier Sculpture Park,
St. Louis, Missouri

Barbara Haskell

Donald Judd

Whitney Museum of American Art, New York

in association with

W.W. Norton & Company, New York, London

Dates of Exhibition

Whitney Museum of American Art, New York
October 20–December 31, 1988

Dallas Museum of Art
February 12–April 16, 1989

At the request of Donald Judd, this exhibition is dedicated to Barnett and Annalee Newman.

Library of Congress Cataloging-in-Publication Data

Haskell, Barbara.
　Donald Judd: [exhibition catalog]/Barbara Haskell. p.　cm.
　Bibliography: p.
　ISBN 0-87427-061-8 (pbk.). ISBN 0-393-02671-X (Norton)
　1. Judd, Donald, 1928–　　—Exhibitions.
　I. Judd, Donald, 1928–　　. II. Whitney Museum of American Art.　III. Title.
　NB237.J76A4 1988　　　　88-28120
　730′.92′4—dc19　　　　　　CIP

ISBN 0-393-02671-X (Norton cloth)
ISBN 0-87427-061-8 (Whitney paper)

© 1988 Whitney Museum of American Art
　945 Madison Avenue
　New York, New York 10021

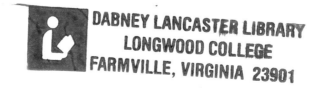

Contents

Foreword

Twenty years ago the Whitney Museum of American Art presented the first one-artist exhibition of the work of Donald Judd. In the catalogue, William C. Agee, who organized the exhibition, wrote: "The breadth of Judd's accomplishment lies, finally, not as the center of a movement, nor as part of an ideological position, but as a series of unique works of high and individual quality." That statement is just as true today. It is always gratifying when an artist featured in a major exhibition early in his career is able to sustain that level of achievement over a long period of time. During the past two decades, Judd's stature as one of the most important artists of our era has remained secure. At the same time, the Whitney Museum has demonstrated its continued commitment by frequently including his sculpture in exhibitions and through the acquisition of six works for the Permanent Collection —five sculptures and a drawing, ranging in date from 1965 to 1984.

Barbara Haskell suggested this exhibition and she has worked diligently to present the artist and his work in the most comprehensive manner in order to reveal his extraordinary talent. Although Judd was a key figure in the development of the intellectual concerns and realized ideas of Minimalism, both as an artist and critic, we feel his work is not sufficiently appreciated outside the art community. For this reason we are indebted to the W. Alton Jones Foundation and the National Endowment for the Arts for undertaking the sponsorship of an important exhibition devoted to an artist whose work is not easily understood or accepted. We are also grateful to the museums and private collectors who have enthusiastically lent their cherished works of art. Finally, we extend our thanks to the artist for his generous cooperation throughout the organization of this project.

Tom Armstrong
Director

Acknowledgments

A twenty-five year survey of the work of a prolific artist entails for that artist an investment of time and energy that would otherwise be spent in more aesthetic pursuits. In this regard, I am exceptionally grateful to Donald Judd, who has generously given his time and resources to this project. On his staff, Ellie Meyer, Randy Walz, and Rob Wilson provided the fullest possible assistance and support, as did the personnel of the Paula Cooper and Leo Castelli galleries, in particular Julie Graham and Lisa Martizia. Likewise, the Waddington Galleries, Ltd., Lawrence Oliver Gallery, Margo Leavin Gallery, Galerie Annemarie Verna, and Galerie Lelong were exceedingly generous with information and photographs; so, too, were the photographers Paul Hester and Greg Hursley.

I am equally fortunate to have had a particularly high level of assistance from my staff. I am indebted to Jane Niehaus, Elizabeth Geissler, Susan Baird, Nina Rosenblatt, Priscilla Vail, and Karen Shelby, who worked on the project in its early stages, and to Susan Cooke, Cas Stachelberg, Lisa Servon, and Leslie Nolan, who saw it through to completion. I am also extremely grateful to Leon Botstein, who contributed valuable insights during the preparation of the manuscript.

Finally, my deepest appreciation goes to Tom Armstrong and my colleagues at the Whitney Museum, all of whom provided the kind of support and encouragement that is so welcome in the profession.

Barbara Haskell
Curator, Painting and Sculpture

This exhibition is sponsored by the W. Alton Jones Foundation and the National Endowment for the Arts.

This publication is supported by income from endowments established by Henry and Elaine Kaufman, the Andrew W. Mellon Foundation, Mrs. Donald A. Petrie, and the Primerica Foundation.

Fig. 1 *Untitled*, 1982

Aluminum and violet plexiglass, three units: 39⅜ x 39⅜ x 12½ in. (100 x 100 x 32 cm) each

Collection of Annemarie and Gianfranco Verna

Donald Judd: Beyond Formalism

Barbara Haskell

Donald Judd's sculpture epitomized the new American art that emerged in the 1960s as a counter to European compositional conventions of hierarchical balance. His reductive, geometric forms exemplified the modernist imperative toward the purification of media which had marked the middle of the century. Yet his challenge to conventional distinctions among media simultaneously provoked a revolt against this "purity," which opened the floodgates of Post-Modernism. As a critic, his forceful and unequivocal views on art established the framework in which his art and that of his peers was discussed. At the time, these views were perceived as exclusively formal. And, indeed, it was the abstract, plastic features of the new American art that Judd articulated with greatest clarity. In retrospect, however, his writings seem permeated with an almost fanatical fervor to rescue art from its attempt to say more than was allowed by its formal limitations. By isolating the essential nature of these limitations, and respecting them in his art, he sought to define the boundaries of what art can express as true.

For Judd, art had an ethical responsibility to express only what would not exceed the limits of empirical knowledge.[1] Rejecting cosmic and metaphysical speculations, he held that the truth of art resided in its visual correspondence to what is known — a truth that exclusively formalist readings denied.[2] Judd's conviction that art must confine itself to "what I know" motivated his formal decisions.[3] Personal predilections of color and form were insufficient; aesthetic coherence derived as much from non-formal speculations as from formal ones. "*What* you want to express is a much bigger thing than *how* you may go after it," Judd declared.[4] Aesthetic innovation is as dependent on the incorporation of new philosophical viewpoints as on the invention of fresh formal approaches. Indeed, it is because art encapsulates the knowledge and beliefs of eras and societies that it can communicate experiences of those epochs and cultures.[5] Judd's preoccupation with non-formal meaning recalls artists such as Mark Rothko and Barnett Newman, for whom, too, "there is no such thing as a good painting about nothing . . . the subject is crucial."[6] Like them, the crisis Judd faced when he began to evolve a personal aesthetic was one of content as much as of style — not just how to paint, but what to paint.

17

Judd's search for an art whose appearances and implications would not exceed what was true involved a rigorous and extended education matched by few artists. It began on Judd's return from military service in the winter of 1947.[7] Over the following six months, he tested his childhood penchant for art by commuting to the Art Students League in New York from his family's home in New Jersey.[8] Initially, he had intended to follow these courses with four years at The College of William and Mary in Williamsburg, Virginia. But his experience at the League had convinced him that he wanted a career in art, and he returned to New York after only one year at the college. Beginning that fall — 1949 — he attended the Art Students League during the day and studied philosophy at Columbia University in the evening. In October 1953, he graduated *cum laude* from Columbia with a degree in philosophy; a year later, he left the League.

The Art Students League, long a bastion of realism, had encouraged Judd's pursuit of a representational mode (Figs. 2, 3). But eventually his philosophical allegiance to knowledge based on sensory experience led him to reject such imitative realism. Judd had, as he once remarked, "leapt into the world an empiricist" — an assessment born out by the impassive accounting of factual details that he telegrammed to his mother on the eve of shipping out for Korea in 1946: "DEAR MOM VAN HORN TEXAS. 1260 POPULATION. NICE TOWN BEAUTIFUL COUNTRY MOUNTAINS—LOVE DON. 1946 DEC 17 PM 5:45."[9] His instinctual belief that only verifiable experience had truth value had been strengthened by his reading of philosophy, particularly of Hume. Hume's empiricism had convinced him that "substance," as something distinct from an object's palpable qualities, was fallacious.[10] Only what could be felt and experienced was credible. Truth was manifested through the accumulation of concrete experiences, not through the imposition of metaphysical constructs. To Judd, the realistic depiction of objects or figures in a naturalistic space was justifiable only if one believed "that objects are so important that the composition and the color must not violate their integrity."[11] Even residual shreds of such a space "signified a unified and idealistic world." And this world-view presumed that objects or figures were physical correlatives of distilled, universal concepts; and, further, that their non-corporeal essences could be understood and depicted. To Judd, the difference between a Chardin still life and one by Walter Murch was one of belief. Chardin adhered to the philosophy that objects contain the spiritual essence and order of the whole universe. That Murch did not subscribe to this philosophical idealism but nevertheless perpetuated a realist

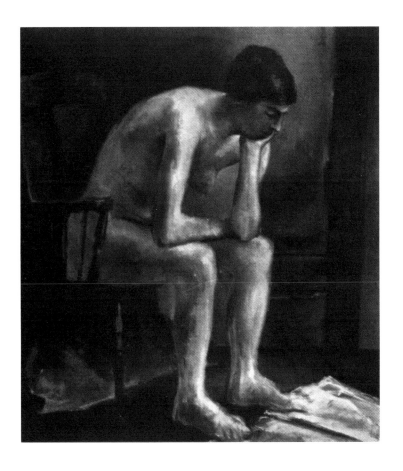

Fig. 2   *BOSA, A.M.*, 1952

Oil on canvas

Reproduced in the Art Students League
1952–1953 catalogue

Whereabouts unknown

Fig. 3   *Untitled,* n.d.

Lithograph on paper

Executed by Judd during his tenure at
the Art Students League, 1952–54

Collection of the artist

Fig. 4   *Untitled*, 1955

Oil on canvas, 30 x 37 in. (76.2 x 94 cm)

Collection of the artist

Fig. 5   *Untitled*, 1958

Oil on canvas, 51 ½ x 56 in.
(130.8 x 142.2 cm)

Collection of the artist

style made his work inferior.[12] Judd regarded Murch's presumption as the ultimate deceit. Even the very implication that observing, feeling, and recording one's emotions about an object said something about the observed object contradicted Judd's tenet that what one felt about things, and what things are, were not synonymous.[13]

Judd's distrust of illusionistic depictions as conveyors of truth led him away from realism and into abstraction. Initially, he used nature as a springboard, much as had earlier modernists such as Arthur Dove, to whose work one critic compared Judd's.[14] Yet, unlike Dove and others, Judd's abstracted landscape images did not entail a statement about nature. Indeed, his unwillingness to concede that subjective states had general relevance or that such states were communicable was responsible for his resistance to Abstract Expressionism. Although he never faltered in his admiration for the formal innovations of the Abstract Expressionists, particularly Pollock, Newman, and Rothko, he could not believe their conceit that private ruminations would tap inner sources common to all men and thereby transcribe shared experience. The speculative quality of such transcriptions exceeded the limits of verifiable knowledge and therefore were not legitimate subjects for art.

Judd's search for a more factual and unambiguous visual expression led him to expel from his landscape images all metaphoric references to anything but the painting's formal properties. Even to ascribe titles incriminated art in allusions that suggested more than was true. The discrete, legible shapes into which Judd organized his brushed areas of paint made no claims to being anything but themselves (Figs. 4, 5). Limited to dark shapes deployed on light backgrounds, their assertive power paralleled efforts of contemporaries such as Al Held and Ray Parker to establish an alternative to the formlessness of Abstract Expressionism. As Lawrence Campbell remarked about Judd's 1956 exhibition at the Panoras Gallery in New York, Judd seemed "to be struggling," but with problems whose quality lent interest to his work.[15]

Despite a reasonably positive critical response to these paintings, Judd realized that only teaching could provide him with a steady income. He therefore returned to Columbia University in 1957 as a graduate student in art history while simultaneously teaching part-time at the Allen-Stevenson private elementary school.[16] By 1959, he had begun reviewing on a monthly basis for *Arts* magazine.[17] Although Judd later claimed that his reason for taking the job at *Arts* was strictly mercenary, the job carried important benefits: not only did the magazine endow him with at least a marginal position of authority and stature in the art world, but his writing assignments forced him to constantly scrutinize and conceptualize developments within the art scene.[18]

The art world that Judd observed in 1959 was at a turning point. What once had been the fiercely liberating and powerful style of Abstract Expressionism had deteriorated in the hands of second- and third-generation followers into academic mannerism. Paradoxically, at the very time that Abstract Expressionism was perceived as exhausted and bankrupt, it simultaneously exerted a hegemony so absolute that it overshadowed or excluded everything else. Judd was acutely aware of the decline and rigidity that had enveloped the New York School. His motivation to chart a new course arose from his uneasiness about the situation and his disinclination to mindlessly repeat the past: "nothing setting us upon the change of state, or upon any new action, but some uneasiness," as he later described it.[19]

The lack of authenticity and conviction that Judd's generation perceived in the work of its predecessors engendered an art form that abjured subjectivity and metaphysical aspirations. Logic and clarity replaced ambiguity and inconclusiveness. Emphasis on objective, literal facts — whether of subject matter as in Pop Art or of concrete physical properties as in Judd's work — became the salient aesthetic traits. Humanist values gave way to a concern with material actualities. As Frank Stella announced, "there aren't any particularly poetic or mysterious qualities [in my painting]. My painting is based on the fact that only what can be seen there is there. . . . What you see is what you see."[20] Such objectivity linked up directly with Judd's insistence on empirical facts alone being credible.

Not surprisingly, given this aesthetic climate, the formalist analysis of an art work's purely plastic or abstract qualities replaced introspective interpretation as the dominant critical mode. But it was formalism conjoined with arguments for the "purity" of each medium. Taking his cue from Gotthold Lessing's 1766 treatise on the *Laocoön*, Clement Greenberg had persuasively argued that each discipline had a responsibility to dissociate itself from the others by capitalizing on the properties that belonged exclusively to it.[21] Since flatness or two-dimensionality was the only condition that painting shared with no other art form, it was incumbent on painters to surrender to this aspect by eliminating all suggestions of illusionistic

Fig. 6   *Untitled*, 1960

Oil on canvas, 70 x 58 in.
(177.8 x 147.3 cm)

Collection of the artist

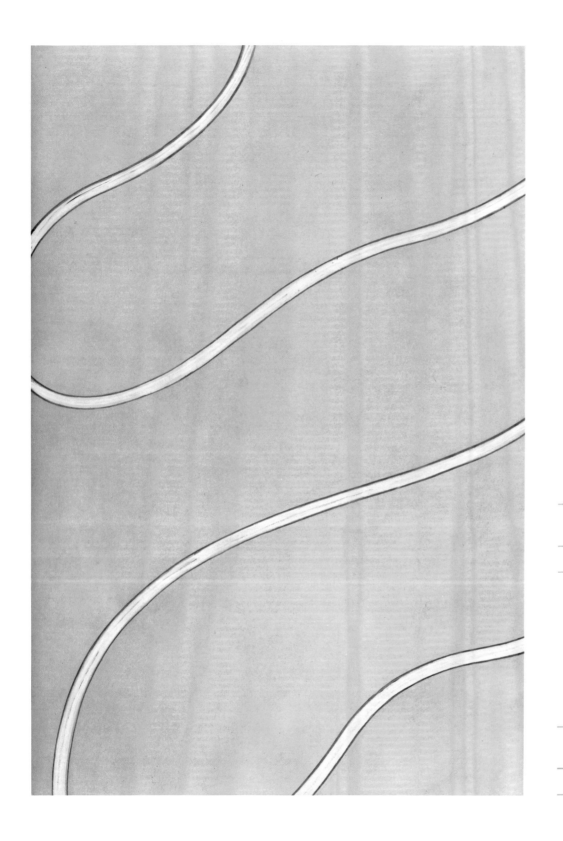

Fig. 7 *Untitled*, 1960

Oil on canvas, 70 x 47¾ in.
(177.8 x 121.3 cm)

The National Gallery of Canada, Ottawa

Fig. 8 *Untitled*, 1960

Oil on canvas, 40¼ x 36 in.
(102.2 x 91.4 cm)

Collection of the artist

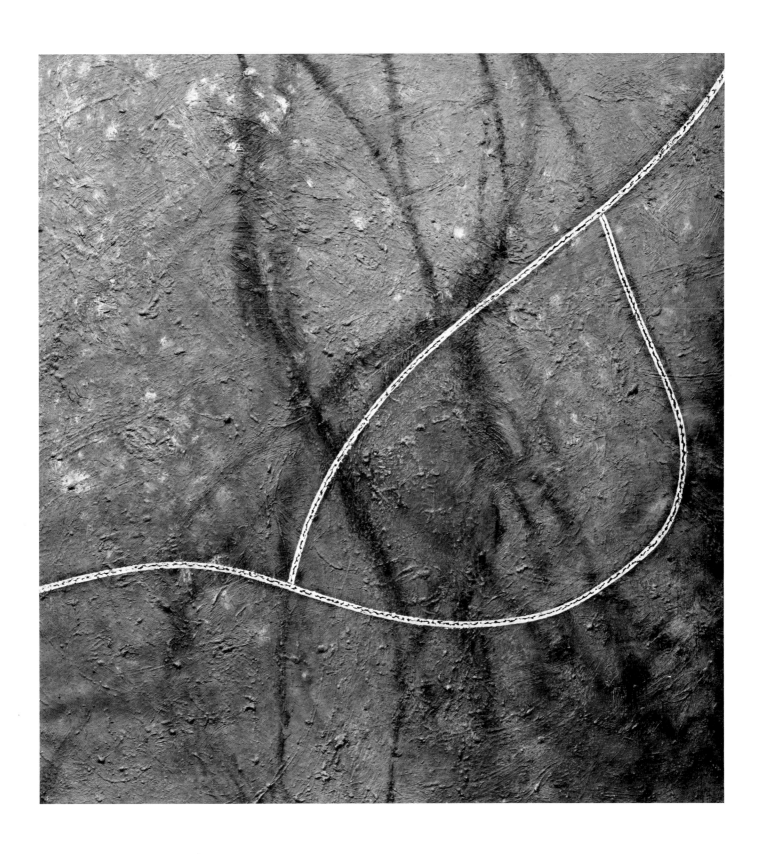

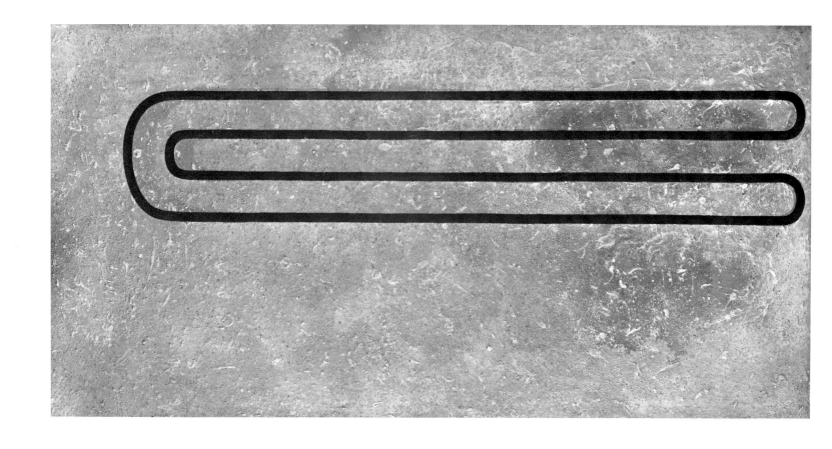

Fig. 9 *Untitled*, 1961

Liquitex and sand on masonite, 48 x 96 in. (121.9 x 243.8 cm)

The Solomon R. Guggenheim Museum, New York; Gift of Mr. and Mrs. Leo Castelli

spatial recession. According to Greenberg, this process of highlighting the plastic properties of painting by emphasizing the medium's inherent two-dimensionality was governed by a kind of art historical determinism; the impulse toward flatness was inexorable. By the late fifties, Greenberg's proposals seemed irrefutable: two-dimensionality as a requisite for pictorial success became prescriptive.[22]

These modernist admonitions were paramount to Judd as he searched for a way in his own work to circumvent illusionism. From the beginning of his career, Judd's aesthetic mandate had been the elimination of deceit and falsehood. He opposed spatial illusionism because its implied presentation of three-dimensional space on a two-dimensional surface was a lie. His temporary solution in 1960 was to abandon shapes on a field in favor of curved lines which extended to the limits of the frame (Figs. 6–8). By loosely scumbling his monochromatic grounds and, later, by adding sand to his oil medium, he attempted to make the surface as palpably physical as possible — to "make it just surface," as he later said.[23] Seeking to purge all residual organic associations, in 1961 Judd organized his meandering curved forms into more geometric linear configurations that suggested machinelike circuitry (Fig. 9). By late 1961, these internal images had become fully geometric (Fig. 11).

Judd's willingness to adopt a geometric vocabulary followed the example set by Frank Stella and Kenneth Noland of an "impure" geometry — that is, geometric forms independent of the metaphysical ideality and purity associated with Mondrian. It was this congruence between geometry and spiritual order that had initially kept Judd from geometric conceits.[24] For him, the implied distillation of reality in Mondrian's Neo-Plasticism denoted a specious metaphysical order that "underlies, overlies, is within, above, below or beyond everything."[25] The overarching claims such speculations engendered were unprovable and therefore untenable.

Although geometry seemed less tainted with metaphysics after Stella and Noland, it still did not solve the problem of illusionism, which Judd eventually concluded was endemic to painting: all images within the rectangular field — even geometric ones that echoed the framing edge — inevitably suggested an object in space.[26] The only way to counter pictorial illusion was through single fields of color or marks, and this seemed unduly restrictive. Judd's initial solution in 1961 and 1962 was to embed found objects into his encrusted paint surfaces in an effort to literally objectify his images (Figs. 13, 14). By incorporating real objects into his paintings, he avoided illusionism, since the shapes provided were actual rather than depicted. The technique owed to Assemblage, whose proliferation in the

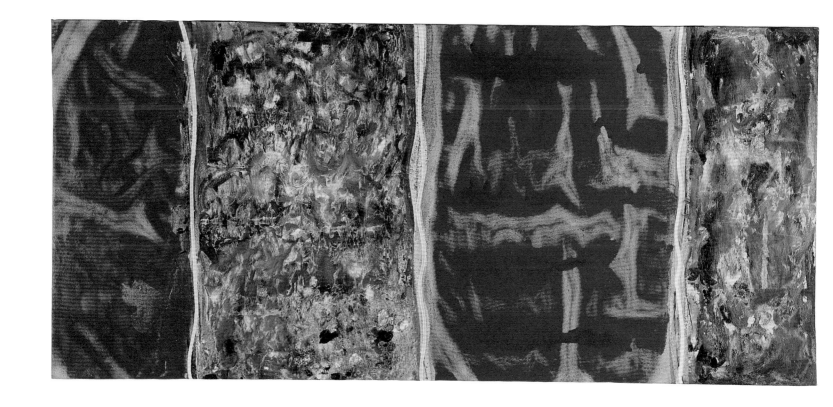

Fig. 10   *Untitled*, 1961

Oil and Liquitex on canvas, 50⅞ x 111⅜
in. (125.2 x 282.9 cm)

Collection of the artist

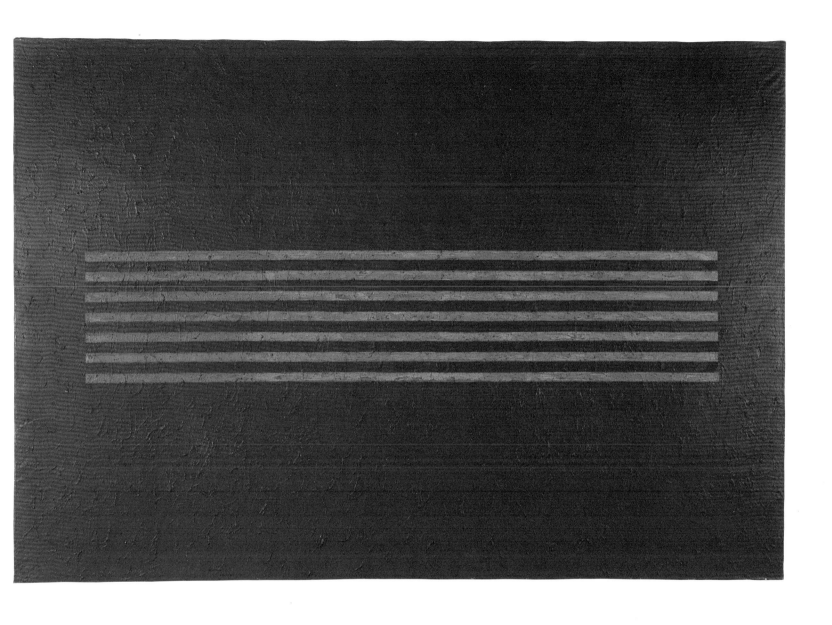

Fig. 11 *Untitled*, 1962

Oil and wax on canvas, 69 x 101¾ in.
(175.3 x 258.5 cm)

Collection of the artist

late fifties had been critically validated in 1961 with the Museum of Modern Art's exhibition "The Art of Assemblage." In contrast to artists for whom Assemblage was a means to introduce experiences of the real world into art, Judd's appropriations remained abstract rather than overtly referential. Nor, despite their dimensionality, did they ever challenge the integrity of the picture plane to the extent that the constructions of Rauschenberg and others did. Nevertheless, Judd's additions of vernacular materials to his vocabulary temporarily connected his work to the then-burgeoning style of Pop Art. So too did his defiance of the time-honored conceit of personal authorship; by employing a "ready-made" image, Judd challenged the claim that the artist's personal gesture was essential to the creative process. He never ceased to impugn the mystique of personal gesture, as his later adoption of industrial fabrication attests.

Eventually, Judd's increasing dissatisfaction with the three-dimensional illusionism of painting led him to jettison the medium altogether in favor of three-dimensional reliefs whose structure and image were coextensive. He found a precedent for this conflation of external shape and internal motif in Stella's Stripe paintings. Seeking a form that eluded both organic and geometric associations, he began in 1961 to attach curved sections of galvanized iron to the tops and bottoms of monochromatic wood surfaces (Figs. 17, 18).[27] By the fall of 1963, when he ceased experimenting with the format, Judd's reliefs were measuring 8 feet wide and extending as much as 12 inches from the wall. Such hybrids of painting and sculpture violated Greenberg's mandate for purity within media—a feature which did not fail to elicit the critic's ire.

The extreme three-dimensionality of Judd's reliefs ultimately demanded a more sculptural format. His first realization of the potential of three-dimensional space emerged from a wall relief, whose large size and shape encouraged him to keep it on the floor for a time after its completion (Fig. 12).[28] A completely freestanding mode offered Judd an unchartered range of materials and shapes not constrained by the format of painting. And, precisely because these shapes were concrete rather than depicted, they were more powerful and assertive than oil and canvas. They brooked no deceit; their straightforward materiality made no claims for knowledge of a higher reality. On the basis of the greater actuality of three dimensions, Judd argued that painting occupied "a lesser position" and that, due to its limitations and exhausted formulas, it was now "not quite sufficient" as an arena in which to fruitfully experiment.[29]

Fig. 12   *Untitled*, 1962

Cadmium red light oil, wax, and sand on canvas and wood, and black enamel on wood with asphalt pipe, 50½ x 45 x 9⅝ in. (128.3 x 114.3 x 24.4 cm)

Collection of the artist

Fig. 13   *Untitled,* 1962

Cadmium red light oil and wax on Liquitex,
sand on masonite and wood, and aluminum and black oil on wood, 48 x 96 x 7½
in. (122 x 243.8 x 19 cm)

Collection of the artist

Fig. 14 *Untitled*, 1962

Cadmium red light oil and wax on Liquitex
and sand on masonite with yellow plexiglass, 48 x 96 x 2½ in. (122 x 243.8 x
6.4 cm)

Collection of Gerald S. Elliott

Fig. 15 *Untitled*, 1961

Oil on canvas, 66⅞ x 66⅝ in.
(170 x 169.2 cm)

Collection of the artist

Fig. 16 *Untitled*, 1962

Cadmium red light oil on wood and
masonite, black enamel on masonite and
wood with asphalt pipe, 44¼ x 40⅜ x 13¾
in. (112.4 x 102.5 x 35 cm)

Collection of the artist

Fig. 17 *Untitled*, 1963

Black enamel on aluminum, raw sienna enamel, and galvanized iron on wood, 52 x 42⅛ x 5⅞ in. (132 x 107 x 15 cm)

Collection of Gerald S. Elliott

Fig. 18 *Untitled*, 1963

Cadmium red light and black oil on wood with galvanized iron and aluminum, 76 x 96 x 11¾ in. (193 x 243.8 x 29.8 cm)

Collection of Mr. Robert A.M. Stern

Judd's geometric, open structures of 1962 and 1963, made out of scrapwood and painted cadmium red light, resembled functionless objects more than they did traditional sculpture — "storage units of an unidentifiable kind," as Sidney Tillim noted (Figs. 19–24).[30] They contradicted all of the ideologies of former sculpture: they were neither figurative nor did they evolve from techniques of carving, modeling, or Cubism. Furthermore, they dispensed with the pedestal — the historical basis of sculptural presentation — which traditionally had isolated sculpture in an ideal, remote world apart from everyday, tangible experience.

Judd, too, disparaged the association of his structures with the term sculpture, which he felt linguistically connoted that something was "sculpted."[31] From his viewpoint, his floor-bound objects took their impetus from painting. Compositionally, they owed more to the single-image formats of Newman and Rothko than they did to previous sculpture, which was either anthropomorphic or organized as an accumulation of discrete parts around a central core. That Judd's structures were single entities but objectlike led him to argue for a new category of art, Specific Objects, which was neither painting nor sculpture.[32] In the end, however, the obvious resemblance of his art to sculpture was overpowering and the definition of the medium was stretched to accommodate it.

By 1963, Judd's sculpture had become more holistic as it evolved from open floor structures into closed, rectangular boxes. Made out of rough wood, these boxes were low, simple geometric forms with little detail. In one, Judd extrapolated from Assemblage with a found metal pipe, which rested in the channel along the top of the rectangular box and determined the shape and dimensions of the channel (Fig. 19). In another box, he exposed the interior by cutting recessed slots into the top channel, which thereby abrogated the mystery about mass and density that normally adhered to closed, monolithic forms (Fig. 24). He determined the widths of the recessed partitions by adopting a geometric scheme of dividing the channel into even spaces, and then subdividing these spaces with one additional partition inserted in each consecutive space. Allowing the found pipe and a mathematical system to determine structure was a means of defusing the metaphysical claims of art by replacing personal choice with an objective contrivance. Art, Judd reiterated, was not a special realm over which the artist presided as high priest, but a realm in which very limited, specific truths could be articulated.

In attempting to isolate and describe the essential nature of art so that its structure and limits could be determined, Judd had created forms which were simple,

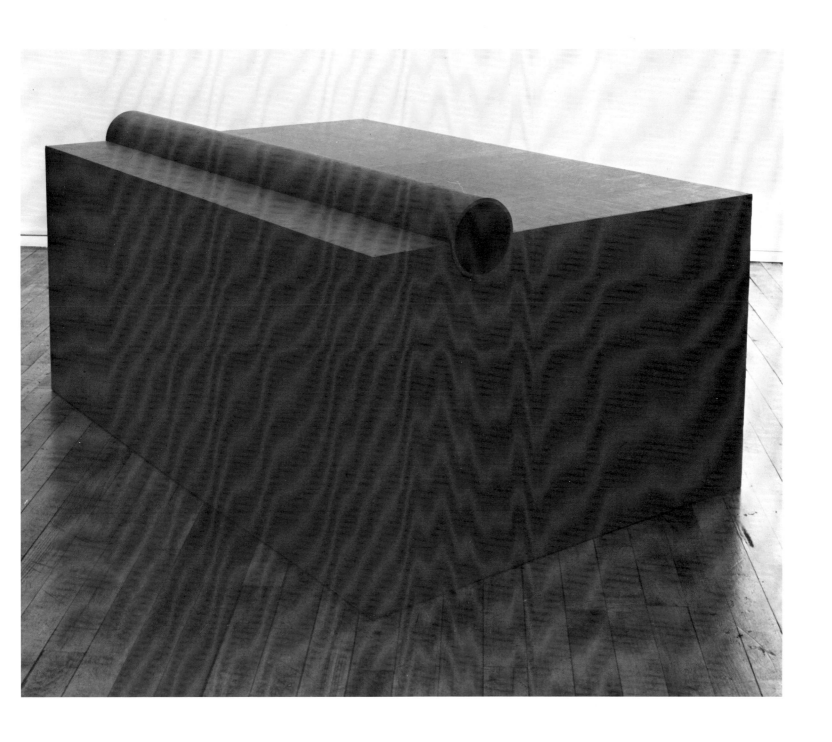

Fig. 19 *Untitled*, 1963

Cadmium red light oil on wood with iron pipe, 19½ x 45 x 30½ in. (49.5 x 114.3 x 77.5 cm)

Collection of Philip Johnson

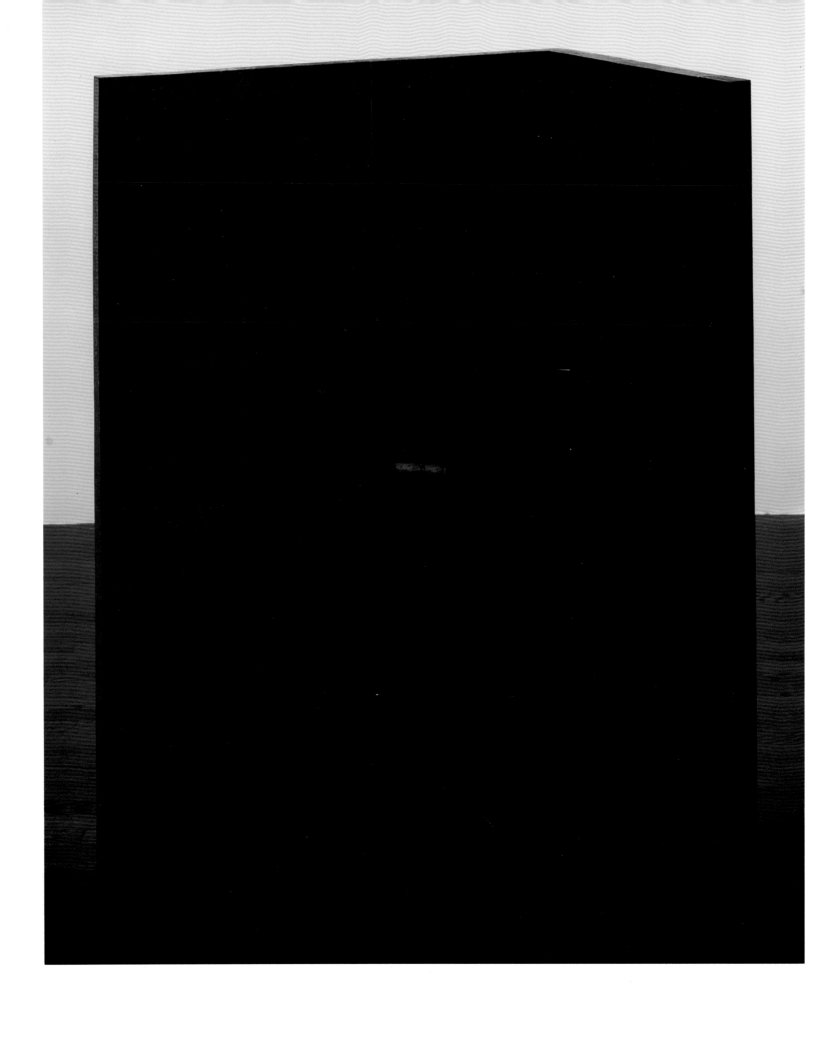

Fig. 20 *Untitled*, 1962

Cadmium red light oil on wood with black
enamel metal pipe, 48 x 33⅛ x 21¾ in.
(122 x 84 x 54.6 cm)

Kunstmuseum Basel

Fig. 21 *Untitled*, 1963

Cadmium red light oil on wood and purple
enamel on aluminum, 48 x 83 x 48 in.
(122 x 210.8 x 122 cm)

The National Gallery of Canada, Ottawa

declarative, and unambiguous. Their specificity of shape, material, and color reflected his conclusions about the limited nature of the truth that art legitimately could communicate. To expunge all implications of an *a priori* cosmic scheme, Judd restricted himself to the objective facts of color, form, surface, and texture since only these could be trusted. A focus on concrete materiality replaced metaphor and allusion. "It is one kind of skepticism," he wrote, "to make the work so strong and material that it can only assert itself."[33]

Judd's aesthetic skepticism reflected his philosophic conviction that generalized knowledge was of limited surety.[34] An adolescence spent during the Depression and World War II may well have contributed to Judd's wariness of all-encompassing political or moral conceits. "There is a breakdown in universal and general values," he wrote.[35] "Grand philosophical systems . . . are not credible anymore."[36]

Judd held that art must be congruent with science, the ultimate model of concrete and verifiable truth.[37] But here, too, new discoveries reinforced Judd's inherent skepticism about claims to an underlying order. The world, he noted "is 90 percent chance and accident."[38] As quantum mechanics and Einstein's Special Relativity theory eclipsed Euclidean geometry and Newtonian physics, science had come to view unified theories of knowledge as provisional and uncertain in an ultimate sense. Science could impose a conditional order on phenomena, but it could not fully explicate its vagaries or reconcile the microscopic with the macroscopic. Even discounting the physicist Werner Heisenberg's uncertainty principle, science achieved, at best, a limited sense of ordered disorder. "Reality," as Judd concluded, "is simply more capacious than any order it holds."[39]

To define the limits of aesthetic veracity, Judd sought to purge ambiguity, for this blurred the truth and engendered deception and falsehood. Only that which was aesthetically precise, definitive, and unconfusing could remain. This drive for clarity explains his initial use of open sculptural forms and his revelation of the interior volume of his 1963 recessed channel box. It likewise explains his choice of cadmium red paint: the only color that he liked which clarified the object's shape by defining its contours and angles.[40] Black or dark colors disguised edges, while white both disguised edges and suggested purist idealism.

Fig. 22 *Untitled*, 1965

Ink on paper, 11 x 8⅜ in. (28 x 21 cm)

Collection of the artist

Judd's cadmium red sculptures were exhibited in December 1963 at the Green Gallery. One critic called the show an example of "'avant garde' non-art that tries to achieve meaning by a pretentious lack of meaning."[41] Pared down to elemental, geometric forms, the work was seen as the culmination of the art-for-art's-sake

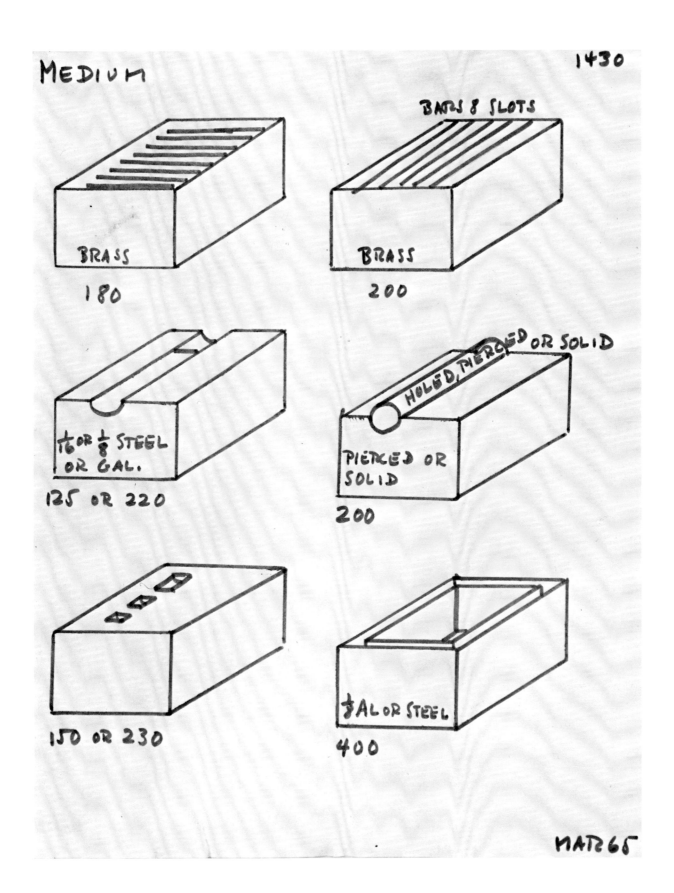

BARS 8 SLOTS

BRASS

180

BRASS

200

$\frac{1}{16}$ OR $\frac{1}{8}$ STEEL
OR GAL.

125 OR 220

HOLED, PIERCED OR SOLID

PIERCED OR
SOLID

200

150 OR 230

$\frac{1}{8}$ AL OR STEEL

400

MAR 65

Fig. 23 *Untitled*, 1963

Cadmium red light oil on wood and black
enamel on aluminum, 72³/₁₆ x 104 x 49 in.
(183.5 x 264.2 x 124.5 cm)

The National Gallery of Canada, Ottawa

Fig. 24 *Untitled*, 1963

Cadmium red light oil on wood, 19½ x
45 x 30½ in. (49.5 x 114.3 x 77.5 cm)

Collection of Gordon Locksley and
George T. Shea

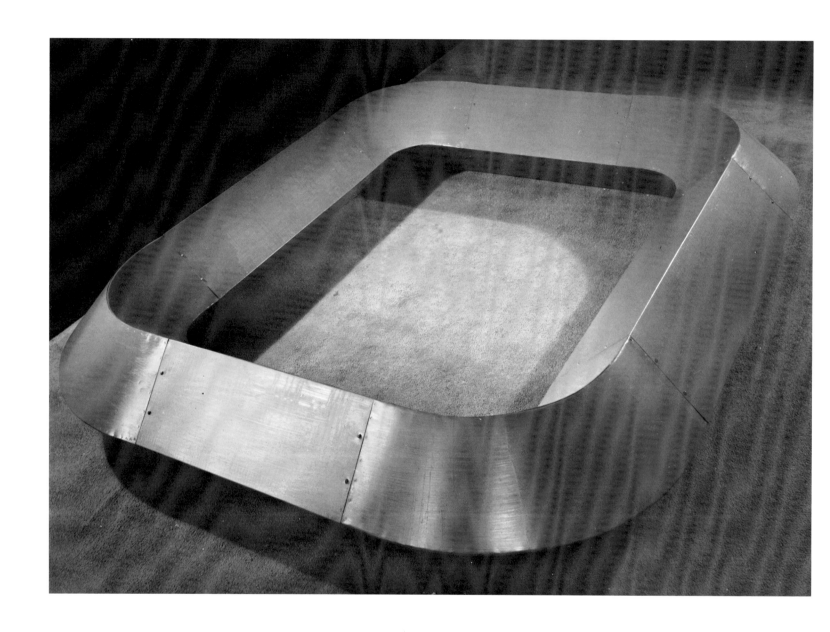

Fig. 25   *Untitled*, 1964

Cadmium red light enamel on galvanized
iron, 15½ x 93 x 78 in.
(39.4 x 236.2 x 198 cm)

Kaiser Wilhelm Museum, Krefeld, West
Germany; Collection of Helga and Walter
Laüffs

ideology that posited art as a thing-in-itself rather than as a representation of or metaphor for something else.[42] Despite the widespread identification of vanguardism with the renunciation of qualities extraneous to a discipline, these works were too inert and uninflected for even the most tolerant of critics. The most flattering verdict was from Barbara Rose, who described them as "our most radical sculpture, if not perhaps our fullest."[43]

In March 1964, three months after his exhibition at the Green Gallery, Judd's dissatisfaction with what he felt was the visual ambiguity of wood's absorbant surface and the imprecision of its variable thickness led him to switch to industrial materials. Initially, he asked Bernstein Brothers, a metal fabricating company, to cover a wooden, cantilevered wall box in galvanized iron (Fig. 33). Disappointed with the result, Judd had them remake it exclusively in metal several months later. The metal provided a degree of lightness and clarity of structure that was impossible with wood. Gratified by the clear demarcation of boundary and the consistency of the metal's shell-like surfaces, he next produced an oval floor piece in steel (Fig. 25). Several months later, he added plexiglass to his repertoire of materials with a floor box consisting of a plexiglass top and sides, steel ends, and an open bottom (Fig. 31). The translucency of plexiglass provided an optimum visual exposure of the interior volume, which became simultaneously enclosed and open. The same desire to defeat mystery encouraged Judd to expose the edges of his subsequent sheet metal sculptures whenever possible through open-sided tubes, flanges, perforated surfaces, or recessed tops. Because such exposures revealed the thickness of the metal, they abolished ambiguity about the volumes that these materials circumscribed.

Judd insisted that the structure of his sculpture be compatible with the nature of its component materials. Practical construction considerations were consequently important both in his early wood sculpture as well as in his industrially fabricated work. Designed for easy dismantling in shipping, his first plexiglass piece was held together by tension wires attached to the metal sheets — a technique which endowed it with a delicate fragility not normally associated with steel construction. The pebbled finish of the plexiglass sheets and the glowing light that emanated from their abutted edges were intrinsic to the material rather than something applied to the surface. The color was thus more "truthful" than applied paint, for it did not mask the material's natural tones. In his metal pieces, Judd either left the material in its natural state or covered it with a metallic motorcycle paint, made

Fig. 26 *Untitled*, 1964

Chartreuse oil on wood and yellow enamel on iron, 19½ x 48 x 34 in. (49.5 x 122 x 86.4 cm)

Helman Collection, New York

by Harley-Davidson, which seemed to fuse with the material and granted an appealingly sharp distinction of edge and shape by virtue of its shiny crisp skin.

In the spring of 1964, after the fabrication of his first plexiglass floor piece, Judd evolved a series of narrow horizontal progressions whose form he extrapolated from a lateral wall relief he had made the previous year in wood (Fig. 29). Projecting off the wall to a depth in excess of its height, the 1963 wood piece seemed unlike either painting or relief. Judd retained its objectlike quality in his horizontal progressions, the first of which recycled the semicircular pieces of wood that he had removed from the recessed channels of his 1963 wooden floor box (Fig. 30). As with the divisions in this floor box, the geometrically determined organization of solids and voids in the wall piece obviated the capricious balancing of parts. This wall progression was followed immediately by horizontal, aluminum wall boxes, visually joined across their tops by a hollow tube which was open on the sides to reveal the thickness of the aluminum (Figs. 27, 28). Compositionally, these pieces skirted conspicuous subjective decisions regarding structure by exploiting symmetry: if the units under the bar were at regular intervals, they were identical in size. If the sequence of solids and voids was asymmetrical, each rectangle and void was augmented or diminished according to a predetermined system of proportions (Figs. 34, 35). The actual system had no meaning for Judd; what was important was that viewers intuitively realized that something other than personal choice was operative. Such adherence to arithmetic or geometric formulas not only avoided the speculative claims associated with personal authorship, but it also gave Judd a means of conceiving his work at the outset as a whole unit rather than arranging it part-by-part over time.

This same motivation underlay the symmetrical arrangements of Judd's subsequent formats. In 1965, he introduced a vertical deployment of seven radically cantilevered, disconnected boxes inspired by his 1964 cantilevered box and his symmetrical horizontal progressions. Evenly spaced from floor to ceiling, the boxes registered as a single unit—a result both of their symmetrical arrangement and their uniform size. Judd altered the size and axis of these stacks in 1966 to create horizontal rows of evenly spaced boxes made of stainless steel or galvanized iron, either alone or in combination with plexiglass (Fig. 32). Although the lack of commercial demand for these horizontal pieces kept Judd from extensive experimentation with different materials and colors, the format of disconnected units of the same size and spacing appealed to him. That same year, he introduced unattached,

Fig. 27 *Untitled*, 1965

Brass and blue lacquer on galvanized iron, 40½ x 84 x 6¾ in. (103 x 213.4 x 17.2 cm)

The National Gallery of Canada, Ottawa

Fig. 28 *Untitled*, 1966

Blue lacquer on aluminum and glavanized iron, 40 x 190 x 40 in. (101.6 x 482.6 x 101.6 cm)

Norton Simon Museum of Art, Pasadena; Part purchase/part gift of the artist

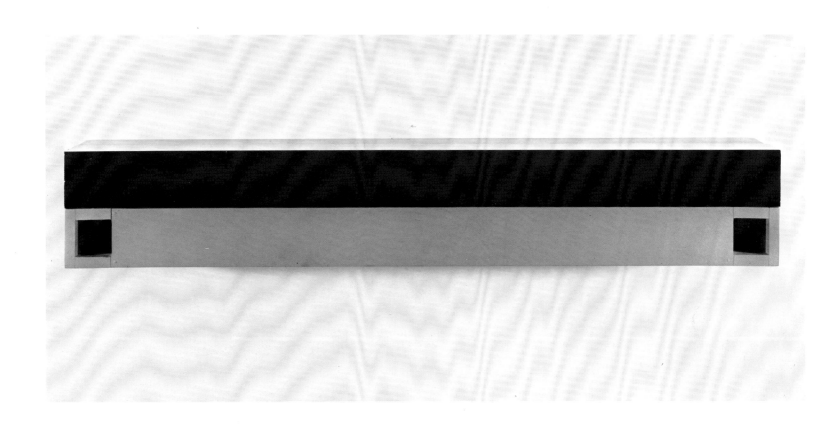

Fig. 29 *Untitled*, 1963

Purple lacquer on aluminum and cadmium red light oil on wood, 5⅛ x 32⅝ x
5⅛ in. (13 x 82.2 x 13 cm)

Collection of Anne and Martin Z.
Margulies

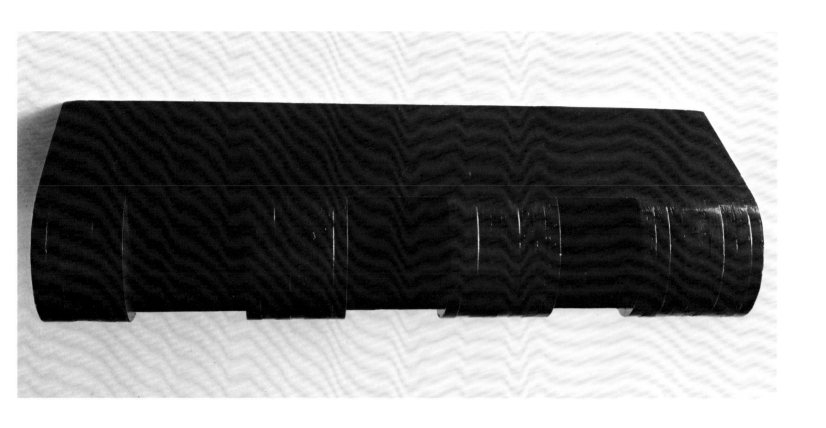

Fig. 30   *Untitled*, 1964

Red lacquer on wood, 5 x 25½ x 8½ in.
(12.7 x 64.8 x 21.6 cm)

Collection of Doris Thistlewood

Fig. 32   *Untitled*, 1968

Stainless steel and amber plexiglass, six units: 34 x 34 x 34 in. (86.4 x 86.4 x 86.4 cm) each, with 8 in. (20.3 cm) intervals

Milwaukee Art Museum; Layton Art Collection

Fig. 31   *Untitled*, 1966

Amber plexiglass and stainless steel, 20 x 48 x 34 in. (50.8 x 122 x 86.4 cm)

Collection of J.W. Froehlich

Fig. 33 *Untitled*, 1964

Maroon enamel on galvanized iron over
wood, 6 x 27 x 24 in. (15.2 x 68.6 x 61 cm)

Collection of Frank Stella

multipart floor pieces whose units were set at equal intervals. The units consisted either of closed boxes (Fig. 52) or open skeletal sections (Figs. 43, 44) whose number and width changed from version to version. The open interiors and wide flanges of the individual sections contributed to the specificity of the works by minimizing ambiguity about their structure.

Because of their industrial fabrication and depersonalized systems of arrangement, these works were misdiagnosed as Conceptual. Few critics seemed to realize that while such impartiality critiqued the excessive claims of personal gesture, it did not negate subjectivity. Judd correctly protested that the creative act was not an exclusive attribute of execution, but could be as potently expressed through the artist's decisions about composition, color, and materials. For similar reasons he disavowed the labels "objective" and "impersonal."[44] Ideas and principles, he believed, could not be formulated in advance and simply embodied in art; the process of making a work influenced and enforced the artist's thoughts, feelings, and natural predilections. As with Stella, for whom the "thrill, or the meat [of the art] is the actual painting. . . . It's that which seems most worthwhile to address myself to," Judd likewise held that what was important was the physical manifestation of ideas which, by themselves, remained outside the realm of aesthetic communication.[45]

In contrast to earlier aesthetic models, Judd's multipart sculptures derived their meaning from the interaction of constituent parts which were independent equals. Neither subordinate nor dominant in relation to one another, they were simultaneously "meek and bold."[46] Like the subject and object in a sentence, they remained uncompromised and unchanged by their conjunction. And, as in a sentence, the elements did not detract from the whole, whose meaning remained of primary importance. They were linked by the verbs and prepositions of material and by the adjectives of color. To communicate visual propositions, elements must be organized into logical pictures; only in relationship to one another do objects and subjects have meaning. To Judd, this was the legacy of Pollock: the creation of holistic paintings whose individual parts remained independent and specific and were not diluted or modified by being amalgamated into a whole.[47] Identified by Judd as "the paramount quality and scheme of Abstract Expressionism," this holistic quality had been employed by other postwar artists — notably Stella, Noland, Lee Bontecou, and John Chamberlain.[48] As with the single, indivisible shapes of Judd's sculptures, the aesthetic extrapolations of these artists from the overall fields of Abstract Expressionist pictures dramatically changed the syntax

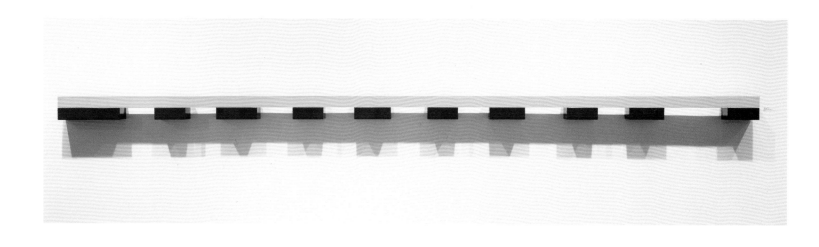

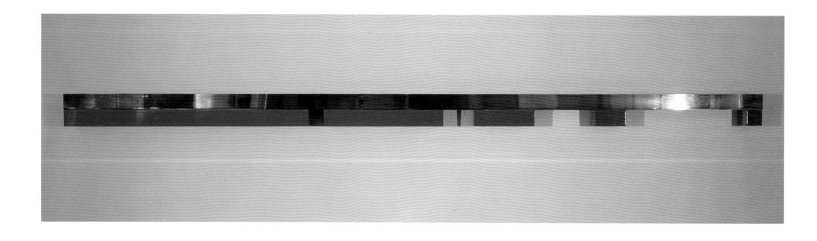

Fig. 34 *Untitled*, 1965

Aluminum and purple lacquer on aluminum, 8¼ x 253 x 8¼ in.
(21 x 642.6 x 21 cm)

Whitney Museum of American Art, New York; Purchase, with funds from the Howard and Jean Lipman Foundation, Inc.   66.53

Fig. 35 *Untitled*, 1970

Brass and cadmium red light enamel on aluminum, 5⅛ x 75 x 5 in. (13 x 190.5 x 12.7 cm)

Collection of Mr. and Mrs. Ronald K. Greenberg

Fig. 36 *Untitled*, 1967

Red lacquer on galvanized iron, 5 x 40 x
8½ in. (12.7 x 101.6 x 21.6 cm)

Private collection

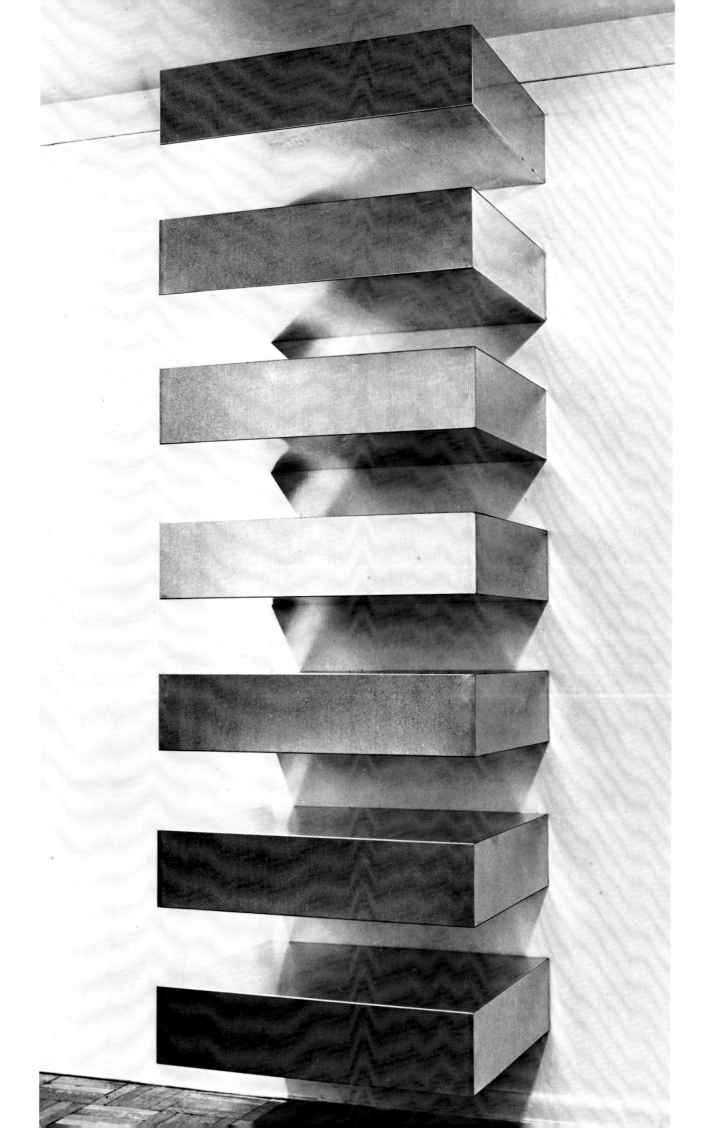

Fig. 37 *Untitled*, 1966

Galvanized iron, ten units: 9 x 40 x 31 in.
(23 x 101.6 x 78.7 cm) each, with 9 in.
(23 cm) intervals (7 shown)

Collection of Gordon Locksley and
George T. Shea, Locksley/Shea Gallery

Fig. 38 *Untitled*, 1965

Perforated 16-gauge cold-rolled steel, 8 x
120 x 66 in. (20.3 x 304.8 x 167.6 cm)

Whitney Museum of American Art, New
York; 50th Anniversary Gift of Toiny and
Leo Castelli 79.77

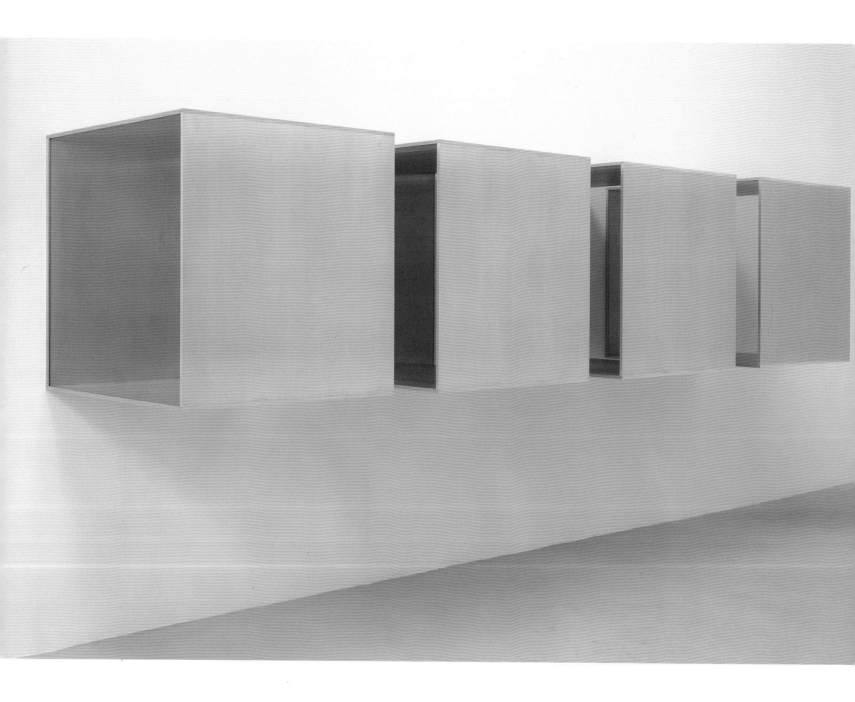

Fig. 39   *Untitled*, 1985

Stainless steel and tempered glass, four
units: 34 x 34 x 34 in. (86.4 x 86.4 x 86.4
cm) each, with 8½ in. (21.5 cm) intervals

Saatchi Collection, London

Fig. 40 *Untitled*, 1967

Galvanized iron with green lacquer on front and sides, twelve units: 9 x 40 x 31 in. (23 x 101.6 x 78.7 cm) each, with 9 in. (23 cm) intervals (8 shown)

Helman Collection, New York

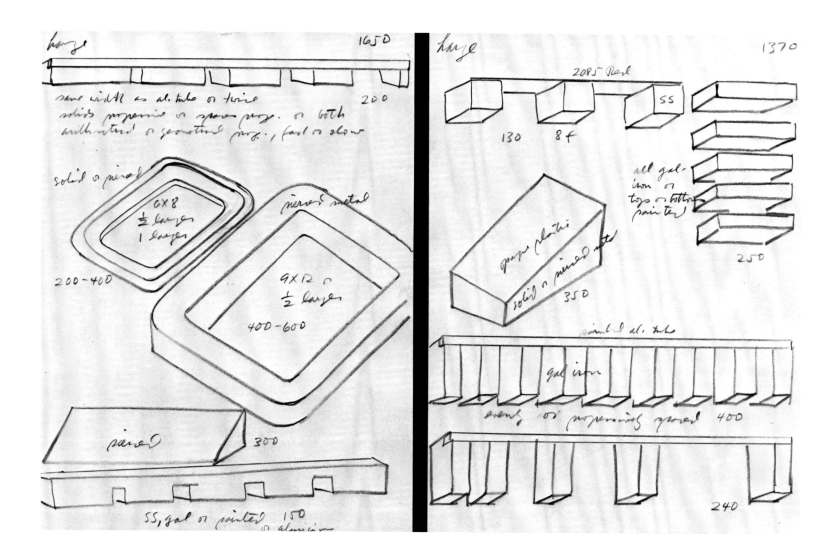

Fig. 41 *Untitled*, n.d.

Graphite on paper, 11 x 8½ in. (28.0 x 21.6 cm)

The Museum of Fine Arts, Houston; Gift of Barbara Rose

Fig. 42 *Untitled*, 1969

Clear anodized aluminum and blue plexiglass, four units: 48 x 60 x 60 in. (122 x 152.4 x 152.4 cm) each, with 12 in. (30.4 cm) intervals

The Saint Louis Art Museum; Gift of the Schoenberg Foundation

Fig. 43 *Untitled*, 1966

Turquoise enamel on cold-rolled steel,
ten units: 48 x 120 x 6⅝ in. (122 x 304.8 x
16.8 cm) each, with 6⅜ in. (15.7 cm)
intervals

Whitney Museum of American Art, New
York; Gift of Howard and Jean Lipman   72.7

Fig. 44   *Untitled*, 1980

Corten steel, five units: 48 x 120 x 20 in.
(122 x 300 x 51 cm) each, with 5 in. (12.7
cm) intervals

Foundation Daniel Templon, Paris

of art. Instead of a narrative semantic structure which required viewers to read a work as a series of carefully composed fragments, here was an art which communicated with the boldness and immediacy of a simple declarative sentence.

Judd's understanding of the importance of relationships in the creation of visual propositions led him to view isolated, unitary forms as insufficient—an insufficiency he noted when criticizing Robert Morris' work.[49] His own sculpture never consisted of only one quality; essential to his criterion for success was the dialectic tension between two disparate aspects. This polarization, as he called it, was a feature of Pollock's work that he singled out as seminal, and it was the theme he cited frequently when discussing other artists whose work he admired.[50] In his single-unit sculptures, polarization emerged from the conjunction of two dissimilar materials or colors, or from the play between the opulence of polished industrial materials and saturated colors and the almost puritanical restraint of the spare forms. Often the polarization was more subtle, as in the disparity between enclosed volumes and visually open interiors which characterized much of his work. It was present as well in the contrast between compressed and open space, which the 3-inch separation between an interior and exterior aluminum wall created in a 1968 box (Fig. 45); and in the opposition between the plexiglass-lined interiors and metal exteriors in two other series (Figs. 46, 50). These visual complexities created by the interaction of simple elements, joined together in a non-hierarchical format, supported Judd's claim that simplicity and complexity were not antithetical.

Judd's juxtapositions did not make general or universal statements about the world.[51] He even designated the terms "order" and "structure" as inappropriate for his work, since they implied an amalgamation of elements according to some general concept about the unity of all things.[52] He had limited the number of disparate parts in each work in order to de-emphasize order, which he felt became more important the more parts a work had.[53] The order and structure of his work, he insisted, had no more significance *as order* than did the sequence of prices on a grocery bill.[54] "One or four boxes in a row, any single thing or such a series, is local order, just an arrangement, barely order at all. [It is] . . . clearly not some larger order."[55] Judd imposed a palpable order on his work, but it was an order "not rationalistic and underlying but . . . simple order, like that of continuity, one thing after another."[56]

Judd's intent in structuring his art so that it did not imply metaphysical ordering derived from his conviction about the inherent equality of things. "In terms of

Fig. 45 *Untitled*, 1968

Clear anodized aluminum, 48 x 120 x
120 in. (122 x 304.8 x 304.8 cm)

Destroyed

Fig. 46 *Untitled*, 1969

Clear anodized aluminum and violet plexiglass, 33 x 68 x 48 in. (83.8 x 172.7 x 122 cm)

Saatchi Collection, London

Fig. 47 *Untitled*, 1968

Stainless steel and plexiglass, 33 x 68 x 48 in. (83.8 x 172.7 x 122 cm)

Whitney Museum of American Art, New York; Purchase, with funds from the Howard and Jean Lipman Foundation, Inc.   68.36

Fig. 48 *Untitled*, 1970

Blue anodized aluminum, ten units: 9 x
40 x 31 in. (23 x 101.6 x 78.7 cm) each,
with 9 in. (23 cm) intervals (8 shown)

Collection of Paula Cooper

existing," he wrote, "everything is equal. . . . These are the facts of existence. They are as simple as they are obdurate."[57] Value differences were relevant only to the individual making them; like time and space themselves, hierarchical distinctions did not exist prior to the contact of an object or person with the world.[58] Judd had substituted symmetry and geometric formulas for the relational balancing of major and minor elements because such balancing suggested an *a priori* "order" which rated some objects as subordinate or superior to others. Because this European-derived, traditional mode of composition involved "all those beliefs you really can't accept in life," Judd asserted that it was "over with."[59]

The compositional simplicity necessary to avoid relational balancing excluded complication, but not complexity. Judd's work was reductive from the viewpoint of having eliminated aspects considered important to earlier artists, but it was not conceptually or visually meager. Indeed, it argued persuasively for the simple expression of complex thought. In defending himself against charges of visual austerity, Judd appealed to one of his favorite Abstract Expressionist forerunners: "A painting by Newman," he asserted, "is finally no simpler than one by Cézanne."[60]

The visual complexity of Judd's work derived largely from his emphasis on the expressive qualities of materials. Between 1965 and 1968 he expanded his vocabulary of industrial materials to include brass, copper, and stainless steel. By coupling these luxurious materials with spare forms, he exploited their inherent "language." The opposition between the inert and rigorous geometry of his forms, and the opulent hedonism and shimmering color effects of his surfaces accounted for the unexpectedly exultant lyricism of his work.[61] It was, as Hilton Kramer noted, "minimal forms at the service of glamorous, hedonistic effects of light."[62] In contrast to painted wood, whose surfaces were absorbant and opaque, industrial materials provided shimmery, incident-rich exteriors which visually dematerialized Judd's otherwise obdurate forms. Reflective polishes heightened the surface's optical quality and subsumed it within sinuous light patterns of vaporous insubstantiality. The complex play of reflections and transparencies inherent in plexiglass fused the sculpture with the surrounding space and furthered the impression of shifting indefiniteness: whether viewers were looking at a translucent reflection of the environment, or were seeing through a transparent plane to a tangible reality, was not easily determined (Fig. 47). By 1971, Judd seemed comfortable in acknowledging this aspect of his work, for he dedicated the catalogue of his Pasadena Art Museum retrospective to Larry Bell, the California artist who excelled in the illusory effects of transparent and translucent coated glass.

Illusory surfaces and dematerialized effects did not contradict Judd's mandate for factuality, for they were intrinsic to the actual materials and shapes. Indeed, they substantiated Judd's implicit claim that every material possessed formal properties that belonged to it alone and that the artist must limit himself to forms that best allowed the materials to speak.[63] Materials were the parts of speech of sculpture. Their properties — surface, color, thickness, and weight — were sufficient to substitute for the role traditionally filled by ornamentation. Applied ornamentation masked the qualities of materials and thereby betrayed them. In order to allow the materials to best express themselves, the structure of the work and the structure of the materials must be closely related. Color, shape, and surface must not be considered as extraneous to structure. They were things in themselves; to conceal or alter them violated their integrity and thereby defied the grammar and the logic of art. To avoid this, all materials must be autonomous and must not imply or be inconsistent with any other.

In honing down art to its essential components, Judd placed himself more firmly in the Bauhaus architectural tradition than in the geometric-Constructivist trend in sculpture. Although both legacies avoided excessive decoration in favor of geometric forms, the Constructivists remained loyal to hierarchical composition. In contrast, Judd accepted the precepts of Mies van der Rohe and the Bauhaus — that form must not violate function and that materials must retain their integrity. In this latter regard, Judd's affinities with the Viennese architect Adolf Loos were particularly acute. Both artists railed against ornament and both proposed the "language of materials" as the key to art.[64]

Between 1968 and 1971 Judd seemed content to limit his formal investigations to the study of this language of materials. He experimented with endless permutations on already tested formats: producing stacks and progressions in several different sizes and with different combinations of materials and colors. Favorite conjunctions in his progressions included aluminum and purple lacquer, purple lacquer and blue or red enamel, and brass and red enamel. In his stacks, he replaced the galvanized iron of his first two pieces with various colors of plexiglass and different metals. Depending on the placement of the plexiglass — on the top and bottom of each cantilevered unit or over the metal on the fronts and sides — the effects varied enormously. Still, while each of these variations had its own specific features, the proliferation of closely related works — in the tradition of Newman, Rothko, and Reinhardt — eventually fueled the mistaken impression that Judd's vocabulary was limited.

Fig. 49   *Untitled*, 1969

Brass, 22 x 50 x 37 in. (56 x 127 x 94 cm)

Greenberg Gallery, St. Louis

Fig. 50   *Untitled*, 1972

Copper and cadmium red light enamel on aluminum, 36 x 60 x 60 in. (91.4 x 152.4 x 152.4 cm)

Saatchi Collection, London

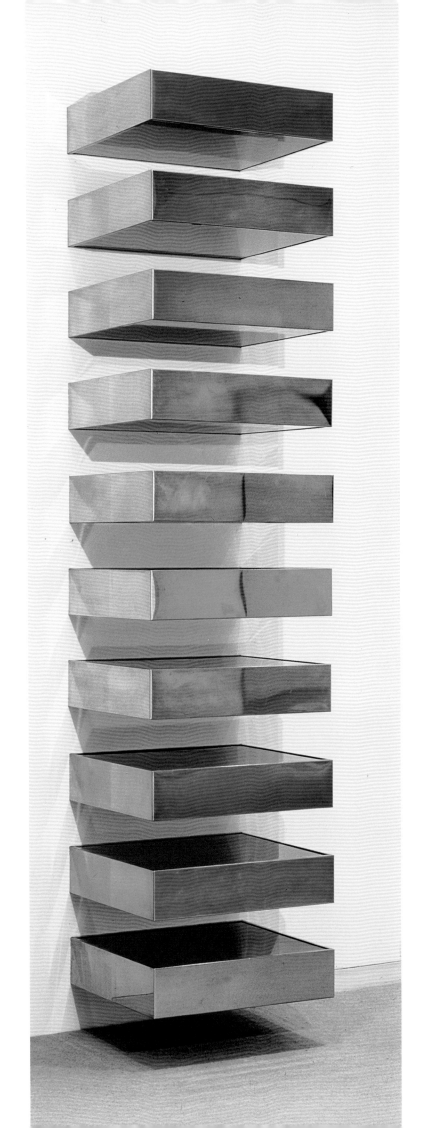

Fig. 51   *Untitled*, 1969

Brass and red fluorescent plexiglass, ten units: 6⅛ x 24 x 27 in. (15.2 x 68.6 x 62 cm) each, with 6 in. (15.2 cm) intervals

Hirshhorn Museum and Sculpture Garden, Smithsonian Institution, Washington, D.C.; Gift of Joseph H. Hirshhorn

Fig. 52 *Untitled*, 1968

Stainless steel, eight units: 48 x 48 x 48 in. (122 x 122 x 122 cm) each, with 12 in. (30.5 cm) intervals

Collection of Kimiko and John Powers

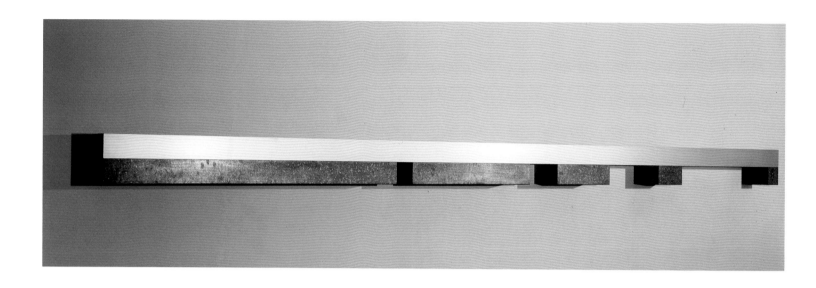

Fig. 53   *Untitled*, 1972

Clear anodized aluminum and galvanized
iron, 8¼ x 161 x 8 in. (21 x 409 x 20.3 cm)

Collection of Bernar Venet

Fig. 54   *Untitled*, 1984

Aluminum, 10 x 60 x 10 in. (25.4 x 152.4 x
25.4 cm)

Collection of Dr. and Mrs. Harvey Snyder

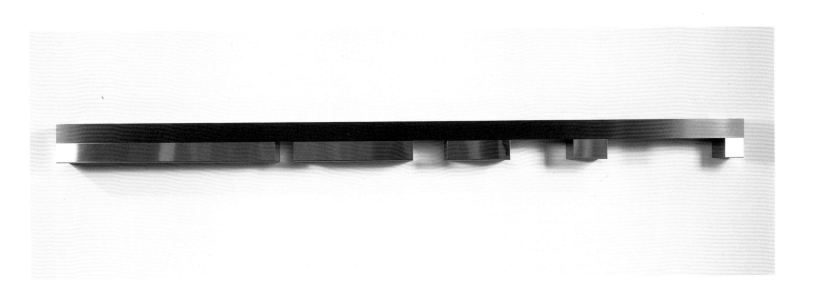

Fig. 55 *Untitled*, 1979

Stainless steel and purple enamel on aluminum, 6 x 110¾ x 6 in. (15.2 x 281.3 x 15.2 cm)

Collection of Mr. and Mrs. Paul Anka

At the end of the 1960s, however, Judd's stature still seemed unassailable. A Whitney Museum exhibition in 1968 was followed by an extensive one in Europe two years later. In 1971, the Pasadena Art Museum mounted a second major American exhibition. Judd's work and that of peers such as Robert Morris, Carl Andre, Dan Flavin, and Sol LeWitt rapidly overthrew other contenders for stylistic dominance of the decade. By 1966, less than three years after its initial introduction to the art community, what came to be called Minimalism seemed to have irrefutably supplanted Abstract Expressionism. Even Hilton Kramer, hardly a friend of this art, had to admit that the show "Primary Structures," mounted by the Jewish Museum that year, confirmed "that a new aesthetic era is upon us" and that this new sculptural expression had "already effected a certain change in the way one thinks about art and even in the way one responds to it."[65] A year later, the dominance of this so-called reductive work was so great that John Perreault reported a rumor that many galleries were refusing any art that was not Minimal or could not disguise itself as Minimal.[66]

Although the literalness of Minimalism ostensibly denied the need for critical mediation, it paradoxically elicited an unprecedented amount of theoretical disquisition. Greenberg denounced it as "too much a feat of ideation and not enough of anything else," and others felt that the concentrated attention the work enjoyed owed precisely to the prodigious critical and theoretical discourse that surrounded it.[67] Max Kozloff perceived so little physical or formal challenge in what he dubbed the "aesthetics of sterility" that he declared the "burden of aesthetic experience is thrust entirely upon the conceptual attack."[68] Barbara Rose hailed the work, but her 1965 article "ABC Art" unintentionally reinforced the conceptual allegations by identifying it as "a negative art of denial and renunciation" and tacitly interpreting the sculpture of Judd and Morris as "illustrations" of philosophical propositions.[69] To Hilton Kramer, there seemed to be a ludicrous discrepancy between the complexity of the discussion and the simplicity of the objects. In reviewing the "Primary Structures" exhibition in 1966, he confessed that he could not "recall another exhibition of contemporary art that has, to some extent, left me feeling so completely that I had not so much encountered works of art than taken a course in them."[70]

The course in which Kramer felt he had been enrolled was taught as much by artists as by critics. Phenomenological interpretations, which were applied indiscriminately to everyone—in Judd's case mistakenly—were first outlined in Robert

Morris' numerous articles. Ironically, the parameters for the formal side of the debate issued from Judd's writings — especially his two articles "Local History" and "Specific Objects." Although Judd was firmly convinced that formal description alone was inadequate in explicating art, his reviews of exhibitions tended to factually describe the physical properties of works and relate them to the modernist concern for purity and non-illusionist space. He might have felt that it was condescending to harp on philosophical ideas that appeared to him widely accepted; or, equally plausible, that their nature was "difficult to make intelligible," as he once noted when attempting to describe Pollock's work.[71] Whatever the reason, Judd's failure to explicate the philosophical implications of the work of his peers was interpreted as a mirror of his own priorities: the result was an exclusive emphasis in the critical literature on his formal innovations. Only once during the 1960s was his philosophy mentioned — in John Perreault's one-sentence dismissal of his "logical positivism" as being "naive."[72]

In his discussions of art, Judd's adherence to many of the central theses of Greenberg and his followers makes his criticism now appear an extension rather than a break with their modernist ideology. The heated disagreements between Judd and the Greenberg camp now seem like family squabbles. Fundamental to Judd — and to modernism — was the autonomous and non-referential quality of art. Although he excoriated Greenberg's linear and determinist portrayal of art history, he nevertheless concurred that changes in art had "a kind of necessity and coherent, progressive continuity" and that the coherence in painting had been the elimination of spatial illusionism.[73] "The image within the rectangle . . . has been progressively reduced for decades," he wrote. "It has to go entirely."[74] He cited the purging of illusionistic space in Stella's and Noland's paintings as "decisive advances" and announced that Stella's relinquishing of spatial recession "makes Abstract Expressionism seem now an inadequate style, makes it appear a compromise with representational art and its meaning."[75] Although he chafed at Greenberg's imposition of a universal style against which everything else was measured, Judd's own zealotry about specificity and non-relational composition as requisites for aesthetic truth made his judgments about art seem as closed and ungenerous as Greenberg's.[76] Judd accommodated a much wider variety of styles within his pantheon of acceptability and was far more supportive of artists whose work differed from his, but he was equally merciless to those who did not meet his criteria.[77]

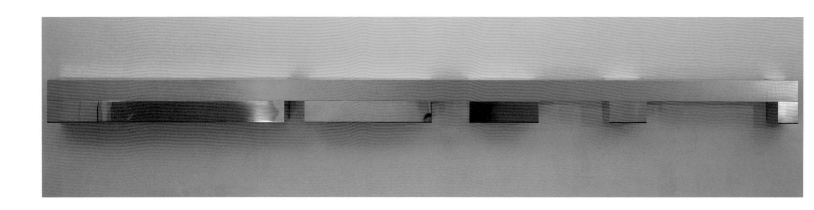

Fig. 56 *Untitled*, 1975

Brass and chartreuse anodized aluminum, 6 x 110¾ x 6 in.
(15.2 x 281.3 x 15.2 cm)

Collection of Mr. and Mrs. J. Gary Gradinger

Fig. 57 *Untitled*, 1978

Brass, ten units: 6 x 27 x 24 in. (15.2 x 68.5 x 61 cm) each, with 6 in. (15.2 cm) intervals

Indiana University Art Museum, Bloomington; purchased with the aid of funds from the National Endowment for the Arts, and gifts from Dr. and Mrs. Henry R. Hope, and the Friends of Art

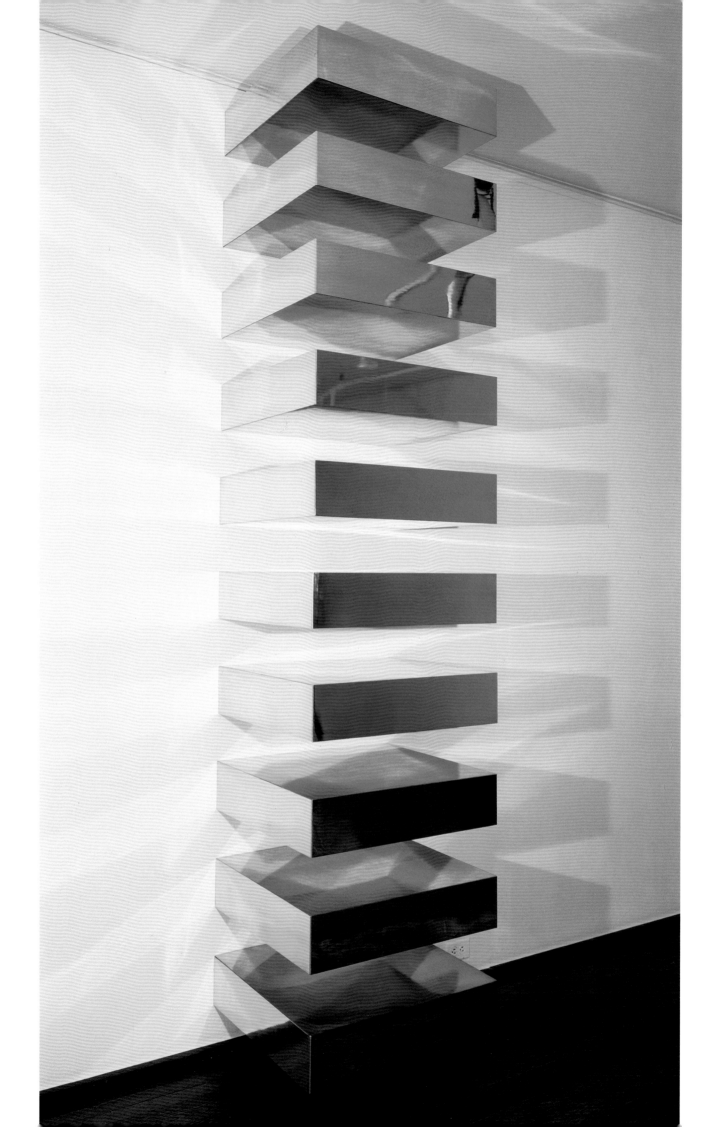

Yet the perceived debate between the Greenbergians and Judd was fierce. Judd was seen as having subverted painting and called into question its potential for future advance.[78] Instead of exploiting its singular characteristics in order to purify and entrench painting, as Greenberg had urged artists to do, Judd had interpreted its inherent illusionism as an implacable deficit and had abandoned the medium in favor of non-illusionistic "real" space. Even Judd's friend Frank Stella felt he had to defend painting against the implicit charge of its demise: "the sculptors just scanned the organization of painting and made sculpture out of it. It was a bad reading of painting. . . ."[79] Greenberg denounced the effect of Minimal sculpture as that of novelty art — a one-time surprise.[80] The more serious attempt to discredit it on modernist grounds came from Michael Fried. In "Art and Objecthood," Fried claimed that what he called literalist art was a genre of theater because it lay outside established disciplines. As theater it was without value and owed its sense of presence exclusively to its non-art quality. In attempting to discredit Minimalism, he fatuously called the hollow interiors of its sculpture anthropomorphic. Yet his view that the art had the quality of "a situation" — in which the viewer "knows himself to stand in an indeterminate, open-ended — and unexacting — relation as subject to the impassive object on the wall or floor" — unintentionally affirmed Minimalism's success in viscerally engaging the spectator. [81]

Judd's art distilled, as Sanford Schwartz wrote, "an arrogant, nervously self-confident time in American art" — a time when locating the boundaries of art assumed an almost utopian fervor.[82] More seemed at stake in those years than decoration or self-indulgent outpourings of personal experiences, which functioned as palliatives rather than as instruments of ethical inquiry. Judd's fierce commitment to ethics extended to politics, which he claimed as a dimension of his work.[83] His art was political, he maintained, by virtue of its compositional antagonism to a priori hierarchies and dominating generalities.[84] "The United States," he wrote, "is still a hierarchical country, sort of a large oligarchy, though apparently not as hierarchical as Europe, which may be the difference between European and American art; my work and that of most artists is opposed to that hierarchy."[85] Despite his opposition to this hierarchy, he avoided specific political statements as potentially hazardous to art's objectivity and wholeness. "Art, dance, music, and literature have to be considered as autonomous activities and not as decoration upon political and social purposes."[86] His desire to exclude art from subservience to propaganda led him to oppose overtly political art and even to disavow any connection between American art's primacy after World War II and American political and economic power.[87] He attributed the upsurge in postwar American art not to cultural or social circumstances but exclusively to "a few artists [who] simply decided to do first-rate work."[88] Although as a private citizen Judd was committed to political activity, he was adamant that art be independent from the social and political arena.[89]

By the early 1970s, the ethical stance of Judd and his peers seemed to some outmoded and utopian. What was called Minimalism spun off into the more rarified versions of Concept, Body, and Performance Art. Overt subjectivity, personal gesture, and metaphor re-established their mystique in the art world as artists abandoned the search for the logical structure of art. An aesthetic of disorder and transience eclipsed the bold and assertive certainty of Judd's work. Even the very rigidity of his materials contrasted with an apparent sense of vulnerability about human activities that asserted itself in the limp forms and process orientation of Post-Minimalism. The precision with which his geometric forms had been fabricated pitted him against those who sought an aesthetic analogue to the vagaries of existence.[90] To them, his work seemed antiseptically cut off from human purpose and intention; it seemed removed from the particulars of life and isolated in a special category where things were absolute and timeless.[91] The pristine execution and sleek forms in which Judd's art had come packaged seemed to belie his opposition to absolute and universal principles and his deep-seated skepticism toward generalities.[92]

Judd's post–1971 work evolved as meticulously as it had earlier, with experiments and subtle adjustments in one format suggesting modifications in others. He did not abandon earlier conceits, but rather rephrased them in new materials and colors. "I don't have a great sense of progress, of change," he once noted. "I like to work back and forth."[93] Nevertheless, a tangible change began to register in Judd's work in 1971 as he redirected the formal imperatives of his sculpture toward more environmental and architectural pursuits. In the process, his vocabulary became more lyrical and less restrained, almost as if, having demarcated the kinds of propositions that art could make, he felt comfortable playing with different formulations of them.

Fig. 58 *Untitled*, 1982

Brass and anodized aluminum, 40½ x
84 x 6¾ in. (102.8 x 213.4 x 17.1 cm)

The Dayton Art Institute, Ohio; Museum
purchase with funds provided by NCR
Corporation

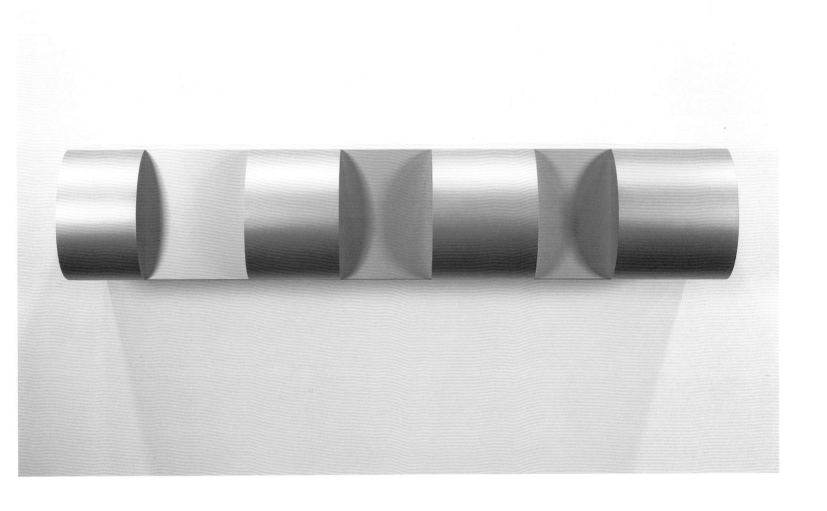

Fig. 59 *Untitled*, 1974

Yellow anodized aluminum, 14 x 76 x 25 in.
(35.6 x 193 x 63.5 cm)

Collection of Michael Rea

A relationship between object and architecture had been implicit in Judd's sculpture from the beginning — in its unmediated engagement with the floor and wall, its geometric formats, and its visual incorporation of surrounding space through reflective and transparent materials. He had resisted greater interaction between object and site because he feared that environmental considerations would encroach on the requisite autonomy of the sculpture's constituent elements. Yet already in his stacks, Judd had realized that structural logic was not forfeited even when the number of units in the configuration expanded or decreased to adjust to the height of the room.[94] He had experimented with a similar mutability in a 1969 "honeycomb" piece, composed of three tiers of open-ended rectangles, whose length and proximity to the wall could be modified (Fig. 60). Indeed, engagement with the wall seemed infinitely mutable; certain of Judd's connected and disconnected multipart boxes could be installed on the wall or floor (Fig. 28).[95] Radical alterations of syntax, however, were not acceptable — as Judd would verify in 1973 and 1974 when he designated two configurations of the same seven plywood units as separate works. Yet, within limits, he permitted alterations in the formal deployment of a work: in 1970 he authorized the rearrangement of a row of 60-inch high sheets of galvanized iron so that they could either wrap around three walls of a room or extend continuously along one (Fig. 61).

The matter-of-fact decisions about configuration, made as practical responses to the site, led Judd to see site itself as a potential means of circumventing the relational balancing of parts. Just as the mathematical systems in his progressions had provided formulas that undermined the myth of personal decisions, so too could site provide an objective way of creating asymmetrical compositions. In 1971, with an outdoor piece for Joseph Pulitzer, Judd introduced this new compositional approach (Fig. 63). The piece consisted of a rectangle of two concentric walls of stainless steel, the outer one level, the inner one parallel to the slope of the land. By juxtaposing two independent systems — horizontality and slope — Judd created a rational yet visually perplexing disposition of shapes. An ensuing variation on this theme was a piece for the Guggenheim Museum, where the outer of two concentric rings was horizontal while the inner ring tilted at the incline of the museum's ramp (Fig. 64). This was followed by an outdoor concrete circle for Philip Johnson: the top edge curved from a level inner circumference to an outer circumference that was aligned with the landscape (Fig. 65). As in Judd's previous work, the visual meaning of these pieces derived from the relationship of two autonomous and equal elements conjoined in an indivisible whole.

Fig. 60 *Untitled*, 1969 (detail)

Galvanized iron, fifty-seven units: 21 x
21 x 120 in. (53.4 x 53.4 x 304.8 cm) each

Collection of the artist

Fig. 61 *Untitled*, 1970 (detail)

Hot-dipped galvanized iron, fifteen units:
12 units, 60 x 48 in. (152.4 x 122 cm) each;
2 units, 60 x 41 in. (152.4 x 104 cm) each;
1 unit, 60 x 13 in. (152.4 x 33 cm)

Collection of the artist

Fig. 62 *Untitled*, 1980

Galvanized iron with clear blue plexiglass,
ten units: 9 x 40 x 31 in. (23 x 101.6 x 78.7
cm) each, with 9 in. (23 cm) intervals (9
shown)

Collection of Faith G. Golding

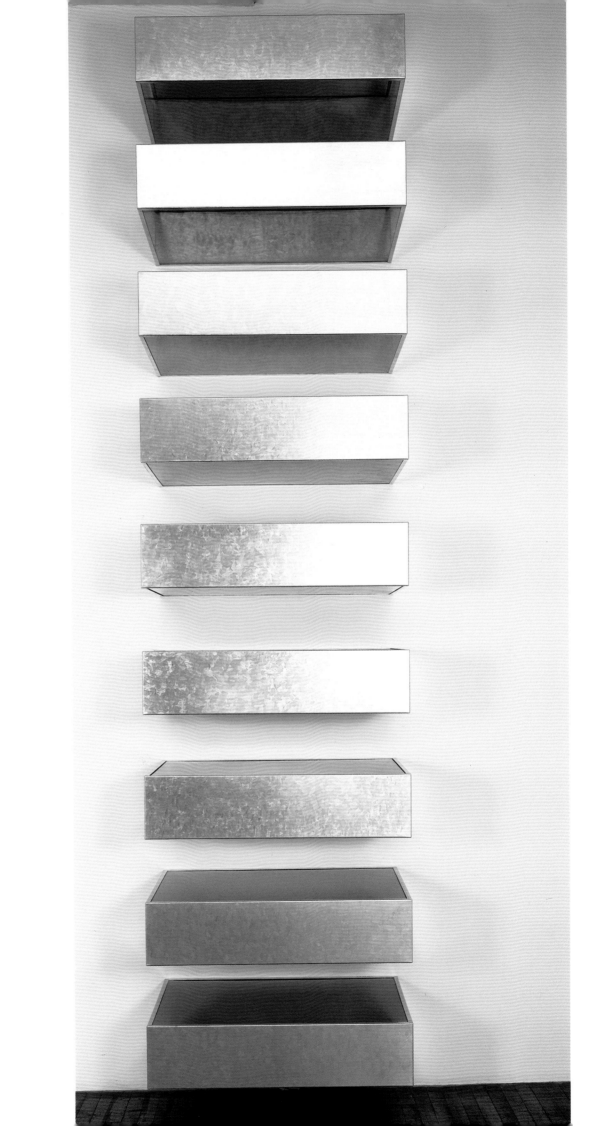

Fig. 63 *Untitled*, 1971

Stainless steel, outer rectangle: minimum height, 54½ in. (138.5 cm), maximum height, 68½ in. (174 cm), sides, 97½ x 145½ in. (247.7 x 369.6 cm); inner rectangle, 54 x 81 x 129 in. (137.2 x 205.7 x 327.7 cm)

Collection of Mr. and Mrs. Joseph Pulitzer, Jr.

Fig. 64 *Untitled*, 1971

Hot-rolled steel, outer circle: minimum height, 24 in. (61 cm), maximum height, 32¾ in. (83.2 cm), radius, 90 in. (228.6 cm); inner circle, height, 24 in. (61 cm), radius, 80¾ in. (205.3 cm)

The Solomon R. Guggenheim Museum, New York; purchased with the aid of funds from the National Endowment for the Arts in Washington, D.C., a Federal Agency; matching funds contributed by the Louis and Bessie Adler Foundation, Inc., Seymour M. Klein, President, 1979

Fig. 65 *Untitled*, 1971

Concrete, minimum height, 36 in. (91.4 cm), maximum height, 48 in. (122 cm); external radius, 150 in. (381 cm), internal radius, 132 in. (335.3 cm)

Collection of Philip Johnson

In 1974, Judd again achieved asymmetrical composition through the interaction of object and site with two unpainted plywood pieces which fit snugly into idiosyncratic alcoves and niches of the Lisson Gallery in London (Figs. 66, 67). Typically, he recessed the front of one and raised the top of the other to clarify structure, but he based their shape on the specific space they inhabited rather than on standard geometric forms. Again, a simple, impartial system had produced an asymmetrically complex but logical form. It was as if Judd had formulated a means of describing the boundary of what could be said in art as a maze rather than as a single, continuous line; art could retain its logic and not be limited to visually elementary propositions.

Unpainted plywood had entered Judd's vocabulary in 1972. Although its warmth of color and complex surface patterns were intrinsic, its soft surface was less rigorously precise and less luminous than that of metal—as if on some level Judd was trying to counter the critical perception of his work as decorative and hedonistic.[96] In the post-sixties retreat from bold, assertive forms, many viewers appreciated the humbleness of plywood because it seemed to reject notions of unequivocal authority and industrial power. Others, however, were less enthusiastic and claimed that Judd's use of plywood was "deliberately designed to starve the eye of anything resembling the decorative impulse."[97]

For Judd, the choice of plywood was practical as well as aesthetic: because it was inexpensive, it allowed him to expand his scale and to explore multiple permutations on single themes, which he had done previously only in his drawings. In 1976, he produced five thematically related sculptures, each of which filled an entire room of the Kunsthalle Bern, leaving only a corridor around the perimeters. Low enough to see over and thus to visually comprehend from any position in the room, the scale of these pieces pushed Judd toward more architecturally sensitive formulations of space.

Until 1972, Judd had resisted making work whose height precluded visual comprehension of the whole, for this would have defeated clarity. In that year he had created architecturally scaled works whose open fronts and backs avoided mystery about their structure. In 1977, he added diagonal planes to similarly open, large-scale boxes in order to yield structures whose dialectic tension emerged from the opposition of two bisected spaces. The simplicity of this binary division of space reflected Judd's long-standing conviction that too many disparate elements in a work would necessitate order which, in turn, would imply an underlying unity in the world.

Fig. 66 *Untitled*, 1974

Plywood, 49½ x 242½ x 71 in. (125.7 x 616 x 180.3 cm)

Collection of the artist

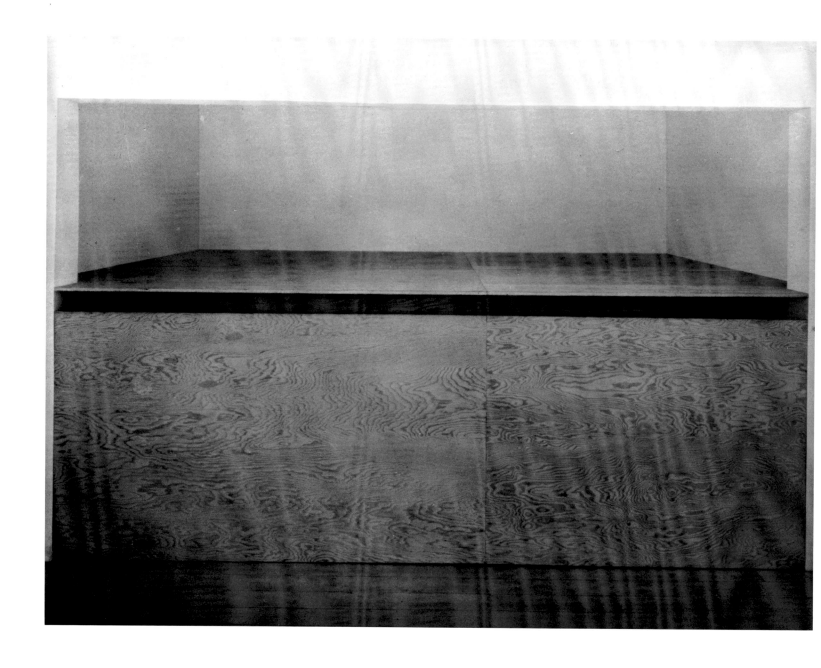

Fig. 67 *Untitled*, 1974, as installed at the Lisson Gallery, London, 1974

Plywood, 52¾ x 167 x 114½ in. (134 x 424.2 x 290.8 cm)

Collection of Giuseppe Panza di Biumo

Fig. 68 Installation at The National Gallery of Canada, Ottawa, 1975

Left: *Untitled*, 1973

Plywood, six units: 77 x 77 x 77 in. (195.6 x 195.6 x 195.6 cm) each

Collection of the artist

Right: *Untitled*, 1973

Plywood, six units: 72 x 143 x 72 in. (183 x 363.2 x 183 cm) each

The National Gallery of Canada, Ottawa

Fig. 69   *Untitled*, 1973

Plywood, five out of six units: 72 x 143 x 72 in. (183 x 363.2 x 183 cm) each

The National Gallery of Canada, Ottawa

Fig. 70 *Untitled*, 1974

Plywood, 36 x 60 x 60 in. (91.4 x 152.4 x 152.4 cm)

Collection of the artist

Fig. 71   *Untitled*, 1974

Plywood, 36 x 60 x 60 in. (91.4 x 152.4 x 152.4 cm)

Art Museum of South Texas, Corpus Christi

In 1977, in an exhibition at the Heiner Friedrich Gallery of fifteen modular plywood boxes that he had made over the preceding four years, Judd explored modular seriality. Each of the fifteen boxes were of the same size and material, but each asserted a different solution and mood. Eleven of them recapitulated Judd's typical devices for illuminating structure through the delineation of edge — flanges, recessed sides, raised tops, double-lined walls (Figs. 70, 71). The remaining four investigated either the perpendicular division of internal space or the diagonal division of this space, which had occupied him since 1974. As a group, their thematic variation within a given module linked them with the serial investigation of imagery that had characterized modernist art since Monet and which Judd's contemporaries — Albers, Stella, Noland, and LeWitt — had exploited.[98] As an installation, the boxes functioned like the constituent elements in Judd's previous work, each one being at once fully independent and fully integrated into the whole. The impact of the installation was not lost on critics, one of whom likened the "majestic and finely measured presence" of the sculpture's layout to the ruins of an ancient city.[99] Kenneth Baker's thoughtful analysis of the installation identified it as an analogue to the condition of human beings — "the condition of being at once as similar and as different as possible."[100]

Judd had posited art as a model of certainty and truth. On this basis, he had excluded metaphysical speculations. Yet he came to realize that the structure of art tolerated more play than he had initially incorporated and that, to be logical, art did not need to adhere to what made visual common sense. It could deny visual expectations and still be fully logical. To express this view, he now set a diagonal sheet inside a plywood box from the top of one corner to the diagonally opposite bottom corner, as if it were a lid that had slipped. But instead of positioning the sheet so that its other two corners touched the sides of the box at equidistant points, he rested them asymmetrically — one-third and two-thirds up the side. Even more than with his earlier, horizontal progressions, a palpably rational system here yielded a visually confounding structure since only if the diagonal "lid" were warped could it have reasonably spanned the box in such a way. Judd had avoided conspicuous subjectivity but, at the same time, had promoted a visually cryptic structure which implicitly challenged the equation between truth and the expectations of common sense.

Fig. 72 *Untitled*, 1978

Plywood, 19½ x 45 x 30½ in. (49.5 x 114.3
x 77.5 cm)

Collection of the artist

Fig. 73 *Untitled*, 1986

Douglas fir and orange plexiglass, six
units: 39⅜ x 39⅜ x 29½ in. (100 x 100 x
75 cm) each, with 19½ in. (50 cm) intervals

Rivendell Collection

Fig. 74 *Untitled*, 1986–87

Aluminum and yellow plexiglass, four
units: 39⅜ x 39⅜ x 9⅞ in. (100 x 100 x 25
cm) each, with 9⅞ in. (25 cm) intervals

Collection of Bernar Venet

Fig. 75 *Untitled*, 1984

Aluminum with blue plexiglass over black plexiglass, six units: 19¹¹/₁₆ x 39³/₈ x 19¹¹/₁₆ in. (50 x 100 x 50 cm) each, with 12 in. (30.5 cm) intervals

Whitney Museum of American Art, New York; Purchase, with funds from the Brown Foundation, Inc. in memory of Margaret Root Brown   85.14a–f

Fig. 76 *Untitled*, 1986

Aluminum and blue plexiglass, six units: 19¹¹/₁₆ x 39³/₈ x 19¹¹/₁₆ in. (50 x 100 x 50 cm) each, with 12 in. (30.5 cm) intervals

Collection of Jay Chiat

Fig. 77 *Untitled*, 1987

Painted aluminum, 11⅞ x 70⅞ 11⅞ in.
(30 x 180 x 30 cm)

Private collection

Fig. 78 *Untitled*, 1984

Painted aluminum, 11¾ x 70⅞ x 11¾ in.
(30 x 180 x 30 cm)

Private collection

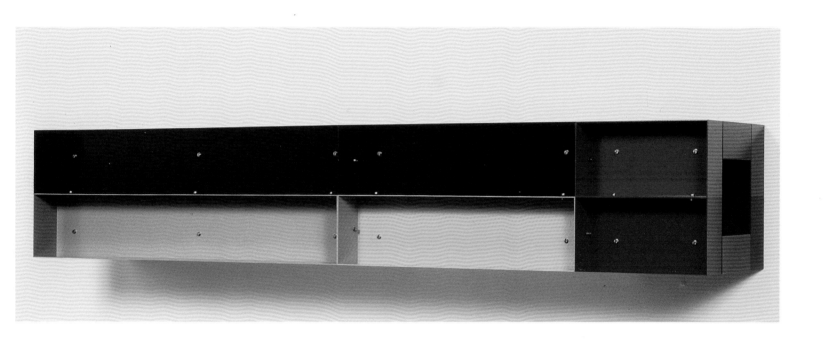

Fig. 79 *Untitled*, 1984

Painted aluminum, 11¾ x 70¾ x 11¾ in.
(30 x 180 x 30 cm)

Collection of Douglas S. Cramer

Fig. 80 *Untitled*, 1987

Painted aluminum, 11⅞ x 59 x 11⅞ in.
(30 x 150 x 30 cm)

Collection of the artist and Waddington
Galleries Ltd.

Judd's involvement with empirically unresolvable structures blossomed in 1981 in an 80-foot long row of triple-tiered plywood boxes, each cut by a diagonal plane slanting at various angles from the upper edge of the front to the back of each box. These shifting diagonals created variations not only in the division of space within each box but also in the height of the horizontal bands, whose dimensions varied in accordance with the degree of beveling (Fig. 81).[101] In a flashback to his site-specific works, Judd employed two independent systems to structure the horizontal and vertical elements, which created an impression of randomness that Roberta Smith likened to the "casual yet highly controlled complex unity" in Pollock's paintings.[102] Here was an ordered disorder that was analogous to the provisional and fragmentary nature of reality.[103] The asymmetrical positioning of the linear bands across the horizontal axis, coupled with the fluctuations in the planes and volumes of the boxes, elicited an illusion of movement along the facade that replaced the static quality of his unitary sculptures. Instead of the simple declarative statements of Judd's earlier work, here was a visual expression which could aptly be compared with musical counterpoint.[104]

Judd probed a similar though more experientially accessible counterpoint in a series of wall boxes whose interior space was divided by diagonal or perpendicular planes in either horizontal or vertical orientations (Figs. 73–76). In some works, he conjoined two or more spatial divisions into a bipartite or tripartite structure; in others, it was expressed in unconnected units which, like those in his stacks and earlier wall boxes, visually registered as a whole because of their modular parity. The most expansive of the series was a multipart piece whose internal planar divisions established simple structural polarities which, when eventually joined in an aggregate of sixty-three units, created a complex pattern of fluctuating planes and volumes.

Fig. 81 *Untitled*, 1981

Plywood, 138⅜ x 927⅝ x 45⅜ in. (352.1 x 2356.2 x 116.2 cm)

Saatchi Collection, London

As Judd modulated the austerity of his structural vocabulary, he simultaneously extended the variables of his color schemes. Whereas he had earlier restricted himself to two colors or qualities in any given piece, he now orchestrated a host of color combinations within single works. In his pre–1971 work, visual complexity had been most overtly occasioned by materials and the perspectival views of his horizontal progressions; after 1971, it had emerged from complex structural strategies. Beginning in 1984, in a group of multicolored aluminum wall reliefs, color became the purveyor of complexity (Figs. 77–80). Composed of boxes with open fronts of various lengths which were stacked two high and one deep around a hollow center core, these works maintained Judd's long-standing dialectic between implied and contained volumes. They adhered to his mandate for non-relational ordering in which parts would be simultaneously "meek and bold," but because of the complexity of the color combinations, the work appeared less systematically straightforward. Color became the main element of visual appeal. The buoyant moods afforded by the color combinations contrasted with the restrained severity of Judd's earlier work. Without relaxing his rigorous battle against equivocation and fraudulence, he had transformed his syntax into more lyrical utterances.

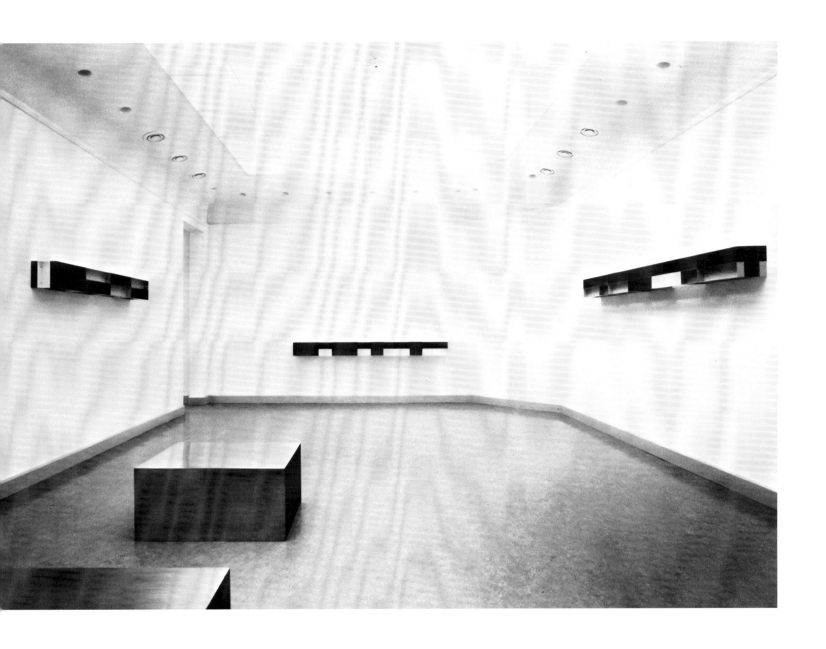

Fig. 82   Installation view of Judd's 1987
exhibition at the Stedelijk Van Abbemuseum, Eindhoven

Exhibitions of Judd's work after 1971 had confirmed the continuing expansion of his vocabulary as well as his stature as one of America's preeminent sculptors. Yet critics had failed to mention his major aesthetic achievement during these years: his creation of a self-contained complex in Marfa, Texas, for working, living, and exhibiting his work. Judd's desire for an aesthetically conceived environment for his life and his art had emerged in 1968 when he purchased and renovated a Manhattan loft building. That same year, his dissatisfaction with the living conditions in New York led him to look for a place outside the city where he could raise his children.[105] Drawn in 1971 to the "excessively perfect . . . lack of vegetation" in the Southwest, Judd discovered Marfa, a sparsely populated area of West Texas, whose uncluttered landscape, dry air, and intense sunlight appealed to his instinct for visual clarity.[106] In 1973, he purchased a block of buildings on the edge of town, which he enclosed with a 9-foot high adobe wall. He turned the two abandoned World War I airplane hangars and a two-story wooden house in the compound into bedrooms, studio, library, kitchen facilities, and installation spaces. Adjacent to the existing structures, he built an office and bathroom.

The lack of high-quality furniture available in Marfa forced Judd to construct his own beds, chairs, tables, and desks. His fascination with the process led him to design furniture for a commercial market. His designs, which had initially been built by local assistants, were now executed in wood by a master craftsman in New York. By 1984, fifteen designs, each available in fifteen different colors, were being fabricated in aluminum. Architecture and furniture must accord with the particulars of place and function in a way that sculpture need not. But although the forms from one discipline could not simply be transposed to another, consistencies in Judd's approach remained apparent. In an echo of the contrast between the incident-rich surfaces and austere forms of his sculptures, he used adobe and indigenous rose-colored gravel as foils to his spare, unornamented architectural forms. A similar contrast between formal severity and yielding materials marked each outdoor area of the compound: the vine-covered pergola with table and chairs designed by Judd, the pool surrounded by a wall of cottonwood trees, and the rectangular alley of grass and plum trees (Figs. 83–86). Judd's only overt

Fig. 83 Pergola, with table and chairs designed by Judd, in the artist's compound, Marfa, Texas

Over:
Fig. 84 Pool surrounded by cottonwood trees in the artist's compound, Marfa, Texas

117

Fig. 85   Three-sided adobe wall in the artist's compound, Marfa, Texas

Fig. 86   Yard with plum trees in the artist's compound, Marfa, Texas

Fig. 87   Three-sided adobe wall in the
artist's compound, Marfa, Texas

accommodation to sculpture was a three-sided adobe wall, built between the two hangars, whose slope tilted in accordance with that of the land and thus countered the level adobe wall surrounding the compound (Fig. 87). It was, as he admitted, "the one big piece of art that tied the whole thing together."[107]

Judd's dream of a permanent place in which to install his work and that of other artists was further realized when the Dia Art Foundation purchased, between 1979 and 1981, a 300-acre deserted army base just outside of Marfa as the site for a comprehensive installation of art. What previously had been Fort D.A. Russell consisted of two artillery sheds, an array of barracks, and a concrete gymnasium arena. Judd substituted vaulted galvanized metal for the flat roofs of the artillery sheds and replaced their dilapidated wood and glass garage doors along the side walls with large square windows, each framed in aluminum and divided into four equal sections (Fig. 97). In the former gymnasium arena, which he envisioned as a display area for two horizontal wall pieces and as a gathering hall for feasts and celebrations, he reclaimed the original linear, concrete floor pavings, and punctuated them with gravel walkways and a concrete floor in the eating area. He also restored the building's clerestory windows and the gently pitched roof (Figs. 100, 101). Outside, he created a labyrinth of thick concrete walls, each with an independent identity, which were connected by brick and gravel paths (Figs. 102, 103).

Judd intended the complex at Fort Russell to serve as a permanent home and public installation for his and other artists' work. In the two refurbished artillery sheds, he installed one hundred mill aluminum boxes which had been commissioned by the Dia Art Foundation (Figs. 102, 103). Each box was at once independent as well as part of an ensemble of thematic variations. Open on one or more of their six sides, the boxes' interiors were divided into horizontal, vertical, or diagonal sections by means of one or more sheets of aluminum. Their lambent, highly reflective surfaces created lustrous and shimmering light effects that changed with the direction and quality of sunlight flooding the buildings. As an installation, they evoked the majesterial presence of hushed sentinels.

As a further manifestation of his vision for permanent installations of art, Judd placed fifteen large-scale concrete sculptures in the field adjacent to these exhibition halls. Each piece presented a different arrangement of at least two 8 x 8 x 16–foot boxes, either attached or separate, and open on one or two sides (Figs. 104–109). Deployed in a line over a half mile expanse of grazing land, the scale and systematized clarity of these works exuded an unpretentious grandeur and monumentality that recalled the heroic markers of archaic civilizations. In 1986, ownership of the fort, a number of artworks, and a large building in the center of Marfa which is the site of an installation of John Chamberlain sculpture were transferred from the Dia Art Foundation to the Chinati Foundation, with Judd as president. Under Chinati's auspices, Judd began implementing plans for the construction of a series of vaulted concrete buildings, of his design, to house three groups of his work which were owned by the Chinati Foundation. Yet Judd's vision of the role of the Foundation was not limited to support of his own art. He activated plans to prepare six of the fort's barracks as housings for Dan Flavin works and envisioned other barracks and surrounding outdoor spaces as sites for the works of other artists that were either owned by the Foundation or on long term loan to it. As the guiding force of the Foundation, Judd expanded his longtime role of benefactor. For years he had quietly supported artists by purchasing work he admired and by using the first floor of his loft in New York as a temporary showcase for lesser-known or under-appreciated artists. Here, in Marfa, he saw the possibility of creating an ideal situation for the viewing of what he regarded as the visual legacy of his time. Here, he could nurture and defend the autonomy of art from commercial and bureaucratic institutions. And here, too, he could realize his vision of architecture, art, and life joined together in a union in which culture was not something "that provisionally lies outside" of life, but was an integral part of the whole.[108]

Throughout his career, Judd never ceased to probe the philosophical bases of art or to question the nature of the truths which art could express. Yet he has also moved beyond the narrowly perceived confines of the Minimalist style with which he was initially identified to create a richly varied and lyric vocabulary. He had demonstrated that a principled and disciplined conception of art did not preclude versatility and adaptability; that an art based on consistent principles need not stagnate in endless repetitions of the past nor succumb to the superficiality of rapidly changing trends. His work stands as a testament to the fecundity of aesthetic invention that can emerge from within a strict set of self-imposed limitations. Judd had altered the visual vocabulary of his age; in the process he taught us fresh lessons about the meaning and ethical dimension of art.

Fig. 88 Library in west building of the artist's compound, Marfa, Texas

Fig. 89 Interior of living area in the two-story wooden building of the artist's compound, Marfa, Texas

Fig. 90 Living/sleeping area, in the east building of the artist's compound, Marfa, Texas

Over:
Fig. 91 and Fig. 92 Interior of east building in the artist's compound, Marfa, Texas

Fig. 93   Cube base chair, 1984

Solid Douglas fir, 15 x 15 x 30 in. (38 x 38 x 76.2 cm)

Collection of James Copper and Ichiro Kato

Fig. 94   Bed, 1987

Douglas fir with clear matte varnish finish, 44 x 80 x 45½ in. (111.7 x 203 x 115.6 cm)

Collection of Paula Cooper

Fig. 95   Library desk with two chairs, 1982

Pine, desk: 30 x 48 x 33 in. (76.2 x 122 x 83.8 cm); chair: 30 x 15 x 15 in. (76.2 x 38 x 38 cm)

Collection of Emily Fisher Landau

Fig. 96   One of two former artillery sheds
which now serve as installation space
for Judd's mill aluminum works, 1980–84

Chinati Foundation, Marfa, Texas

Fig. 97   One of two former artillery sheds which now serve as installation space for Judd's mill aluminum works, 1980–84

Chinati Foundation, Marfa, Texas

Fig. 98   Labyrinth of adobe walls adjacent to arena

Chinati Foundation, Marfa, Texas

Fig. 99 Picnic table and chairs within
labyrinth of adobe walls adjacent to arena

Chinati Foundation, Marfa, Texas

Fig. 100 Interior of arena

Chinati Foundation, Marfa, Texas

Fig. 101 Interior of arena

Chinati Foundation, Marfa, Texas

Fig. 102   Installation of Judd's aluminum works, 1980–84

41 x 51 x 72 in. (104 x 129.5 x 182.8 cm) each

Chinati Foundation, Marfa, Texas

Fig. 103 Installation of Judd's mill aluminum works, 1980–84

41 x 51 x 72 in. (104 x 129.5 x 182.8 cm) each

Chinati Foundation, Marfa, Texas

Fig. 104   Installation of fifteen works,
each composed of concrete modules

Chinati Foundation, Marfa, Texas

Fig. 105   View of concrete works

Chinati Foundation, Marfa, Texas

Fig. 106 Installation of one of Judd's fifteen concrete works

Six units: 98$^{7}/_{16}$ x 98$^{7}/_{16}$ x 196$^{7}/_{8}$ in. (250 x 250 x 500 cm) each

Chinati Foundation, Marfa, Texas

Fig. 107 Installation of one of Judd's
fifteen concrete works

Three units: 98⁷⁄₁₆ x 98⁷⁄₁₆ x 196⁷⁄₈ in. (250
x 250 x 500 cm) each

Chinati Foundation, Marfa, Texas

Fig. 108   Installation of one of Judd's fifteen concrete works

Three units: 98⁷⁄₁₆ x 98⁷⁄₁₆ x 196⁷⁄₈ in. (250
x 250 x 500 cm) each

Chinati Foundation, Marfa, Texas

Fig. 109   Installation of Judd's concrete works

Chinati Foundation, Marfa, Texas

Notes

Complete Writings 1959–1975 refers to Donald Judd, *Complete Writings 1959–1975: Gallery Reviews, Book Reviews, Articles, Letters to the Editor, Reports, Statements, Complaints* (Halifax: The Press of the Nova Scotia College of Art and Design; New York: New York University Press, 1975).

Complete Writings 1975–1986 refers to Donald Judd, *Complete Writings 1975–1986* (Eindhoven, The Netherlands: Stedelijk Van Abbemuseum, 1987).

1. See *Donald Judd*, exhibition catalogue, Galerie Maeght Lelong, Paris, as *Repères: Cahiers d'Art Contemporain*, no. 36 (1987), p. 9.

2. See Judd's statement that "there is no form that can be form without meaning, quality, and feeling. . . . It's a mistaken service to art to argue for pure form; it denies meaning to art"; ibid., p. 10.

3. Quoted in "Don Judd: An Interview with John Coplans," in *Don Judd*, exhibition catalogue, Pasadena Art Museum, 1971, p. 32. Judd reiterated that "art should have appearances and implications that correspond to what is now known"; "Yale Lecture" (September 20, 1983), *Res: Anthropology and Aesthetics*, nos. 7–8 (Spring – Autumn 1984), p. 153.

4. Quoted in Bruce Glaser, "Questions to Stella and Judd," *Art News*, 65 (September 1966), p. 57.

5. "The experience of another time and society . . . can nevertheless, almost uniquely, be gained through art"; quoted in Judd, "Yale Lecture," p. 153.

6. Quoted in Irving Sandler, *The Triumph of American Painting* (New York: Harper & Row, 1970), p. 62.

7. Judd enlisted in the United States Army in June 1946, after graduation from Westwood High School, New Jersey. He served in the U.S. Army Corps of Engineers in Korea until late 1947.

8. As a child, Judd searched out and read all those sections from the *Book of Knowledge* that pertained to art. At eleven, his parents enrolled him in a private art class and he began working with pastels and watercolors; see Roberta Smith, in *Donald Judd: Catalogue Raisonné of Paintings, Objects, and Wood-Blocks 1960–1974*, exhibition catalogue, The National Gallery of Canada, Ottawa, 1975, p. 4.

9. Quoted in Judd, "A Portrait of the Artist as His Own Man," *House and Garden*, 157 (April 1985), p. 156; *Complete Writings 1975–1986*, p. 96.

10. See Judd's discussion of Hume in "Walter Murch," *Arts Magazine*, 37 (February 1963), p. 46; *Complete Writings 1959–1975*, p. 72. Judd's inclination toward Hume's empiricism was supported by the empiricist orientation of the philosophy department of Columbia University.

11. Judd, "Walter Murch," p. 46; *Complete Writings 1959–1975*, p. 72. The next passage quoted in the text is from Judd, "George Segal," *Arts Magazine*, 36 (September 1962), p. 55; *Complete Writings 1959–1975*, p. 59. For a discussion of the relationship between illusionistic space and philosophical idealism, see Rosalind Krauss, *Passages in Modern Sculpture* (New York: The Viking Press, 1977), pp. 254–70.

12. "Not only is it impossible to believe in this technique and space, this treatment of objects; it is not even possible to believe that Murch believes in it"; see Judd, "Walter Murch," p. 46; *Complete Writings 1959–1975*, p. 72. The philosophical theory that an object contained the secrets of the world originated with Leibniz. It received poetic form from William Blake, among others, who wrote about seeing "the world in a grain of sand" ("Auguries of Innocence").

13. "Obviously what you feel and what things are aren't the same"; Donald Judd, "Jackson Pollock," *Arts Magazine*, 41 (April 1967), p. 34; *Complete Writings 1959–1975*, p. 195.

14. James R. Mellow, "In the Galleries: Don Judd and Nathan Raisen," *Arts*, 30 (September 1956), p. 58.

15. Lawrence Campbell, "Reviews and Previews: Judd and Raisen," *Art News*, 55 (September 1956), p. 17.

16. Judd taught at the Allen-Stevenson School part-time for four years, from 1957 until 1961. Earlier jobs included teaching art at a settlement house (Christadora House) and at the Police Athletic League of New York.

17. In the summer of 1961, Judd was fired from *Arts* by Hilton Kramer because there were to be fewer reviews. In 1962, he was rehired by executive editor James Mellow at the now renamed *Arts Magazine,* writing approximately fifteen reviews a month until 1965.

18. Judd also had to articulate developments in contemporary art for the gallery-tour course "New York Galleries" that he taught at The Brooklyn Museum Art School from fall 1962 to spring 1964.

19. Judd, "Specific Objects," *Arts Yearbook 8* (1965), p. 74; *Complete Writings 1959–1975,* p. 181. In a conversation with the author, August 8, 1988, Judd attributed this passage to John Locke.

20. Quoted in Glaser, "Questions to Stella and Judd," p. 58.

21. Clement Greenberg, "Towards a Newer Laocoön," *Partisan Review,* 7 (July – August 1940), p. 305: "Emphasize the medium and its difficulties, and at once the purely plastic, the proper, values of visual art come to the fore."

22. Even the blatant subject matter of Pop Art was discussed primarily in terms of its anti-illusionistic space; it was not until appropriated media images were seen as a means of creating explicitly two-dimensional space that Pop Art was fully welcomed by the critical community.

23. Quoted in "Don Judd: An Interview with John Coplans," p. 21.

24. "'Spiritual' art, high art is made by those who have sufficient information to be 'spiritual,' which is no longer the case in any of the religions, or in the case of the belief in the national state. It's easy to believe or to invent something general if there's little reality to consider or rec-oncile"; Donald Judd, "Two Contemporary Artists Comment," *Art Journal,* 41 (Fall 1981), p. 250; *Complete Writings 1959–1975,* p. 18.

25. To Judd, this was "the sense of order of Thomist Christianity and of the rationalistic philosophy which developed from it." It was these "destructive" assumptions that he wanted to avoid; see Judd in "Portofolio: 4 Sculptors," *Perspecta,* 11 (1967), p. 44; *Complete Writings 1959–1975,* p. 196.

26. Judd, "Specific Objects," p. 77; *Complete Writings 1959–1975,* p. 182.

27. Judd apparently was dissatisfied with his success in circumventing geometric and organic associations, for he wrote in 1968 that "A form that's neither geometric nor organic would be a great discovery"; quoted in Lucy R. Lippard, "Homage to the Square," *Art in America,* 55 (July – August 1967), p. 56.

28. Judd described his move from relief to sculpture: "First, I did the pipe relief [Fig. 12] and kept it on the floor. It was a big thing when sitting on the floor. I left it on the floor, and that didn't seem to bother it much. It was meant to go on the wall, but it looked all right on the floor. And then the whole situation of the wall was tiresome, but I was also tired of low relief. . . . And I didn't want it to sit back against the wall. A piece that was completely three-dimensional was a big event for me"; quoted in "Don Judd: An Interview with John Coplans," pp. 21–23.

29. Donald Judd, "Kenneth Noland," *Arts Magazine,* 37 (September 1963), pp. 53–54; *Complete Writings 1959–1975,* p. 93.

30. Sidney Tillim, "The New Avant-Garde," *Arts Magazine,* 38 (February 1964), p. 20.

31. Judd, "Specific Objects," pp. 77–78; *Complete Writings 1959–1975,* pp. 181–84. Judd reiterated his disclaimer regarding sculpture as late as 1976; see Phyllis Tuchman, "Minimalism and Critical Response," *Artforum,* 15 (May 1977), p. 27.

32. Judd, "Specific Objects," p. 78; *Complete Writings 1959–1975,* p. 183.

33. Donald Judd, "Lee Bontecou," *Arts Magazine,* 39 (April 1965), p. 20; *Complete Writings 1959–1975,* p. 179.

34. Judd, "Yale Lecture," p. 150: "Knowledge is very uncertain and fragmentary."

35. Quoted in "Vanity Fair: The New York Art Scene," *Newsweek,* January 4, 1965, p. 59.

36. Judd, "Yale Lecture," p. 154.

37. For art's congruence with science, see ibid., p. 151.

38. Glaser, "Questions to Stella and Judd," p. 58.

39. Quoted in Philip Johnson, "Young Artists at the Fair and at Lincoln Center," *Art in America,* 52 (August 1964), p. 117.

40. "Don Judd: An Interview with John Coplans," p. 25.

41. John Canaday, "Art: 'Images of Praise' in Three Dimensions," *The New York Times,* December 21, 1963, p. D20.

42. Irving Sandler, "The New Cool-Art," *Art in America,* 53 (January 1965), p. 101.

43. Barbara Rose, "Looking at American Sculpture," *Artforum,* 3 (February 1965), p. 34.

44. For Judd's objections to these labels, see "Yale Lecture," p. 153.

45. For the Stella passage, see William S. Rubin, *Frank Stella,* exhibition catalogue, The Museum of Modern Art, New York, 1970, p. 37. For Judd's discussion of the "first and primary" role played by process, see Donald Judd in *Repères,* pp. 9–10.

46. Judd, "A Portrait of the Artist as His Own Man," p. 156; *Complete Writings 1975–1986,* p. 101.

47. Judd, "Jackson Pollock," p. 34; *Complete Writings 1959–1975*, p. 195.

48. Judd, "Local History," *Arts Yearbook 7* (1964), p. 28; *Complete Writings 1959–1975*, p. 151.

49. Donald Judd, "Black, White and Gray," *Arts Magazine,* 38 (March 1964), p. 50; *Complete Writings 1959–1975*, p. 117.

50. Regarding Pollock's work, Judd wrote: "The elements and aspects of Pollock's paintings are polarized rather than amalgamated. The work doesn't have the moderated *a priori* generality usual in paintings. Everything is fairly independent and specific"; "Jackson Pollock," p. 34; *Complete Writings 1959–1975*, p. 195. Judd reiterated this notion in 1983: "The level of quality of a work can usually be established by the extent of the polarity between its generality and particularity"; "Yale Lecture," p. 153.

51. He "didn't want work that was general or universal in the usual sense"; Judd, "Portfolio: 4 Sculptors," p. 44; *Complete Writings 1959–1975*, p. 196.

52. Ibid.

53. Glaser, "Questions to Stella and Judd," p. 58.

54. Grace Glueck, "A Box Is a Box Is a Box," *The New York Times*, March 10, 1968, p. D23.

55. Judd, "Portfolio: 4 Sculptors," p. 44; *Complete Writings 1959–1975*, p. 196.

56. Judd, "Specific Objects," p. 77; *Complete Writings 1959–1975*, p. 184.

57. "Things that exist exist, and everything is on their side. They're here, which is pretty puzzling. Nothing can be said of things that don't exist. Things exist in the same way if that is all that is considered—which may be because we feel that is what the word means or both. Everything is equal, just existing, and the values and interests they have are only adventitious"; Judd, "Black, White and Gray," p. 50; *Complete Writings 1959–1975*, p. 117.

58. "Time and space don't exist; they are made by events and positions"; Judd, "Two Contemporary Artists Comment," p. 250; *Complete Writings 1975–1986*, p. 17.

59. Glaser, "Questions to Stella and Judd," pp. 57, 60.

60. Judd, "Specific Objects," p. 78; *Complete Writings 1959–1975*, p. 184.

61. Judd described Josef Albers' work in similar terms: the "central lyric and exultant ambiguity" was derived from its "unbounded color" and the apparent rigidity of its geometry; Judd, "In the Galleries," *Arts*, 34 (December 1959), p. 56; *Collected Writings 1959–1975*, p. 6. Albers remained an impressive model for Judd; in 1977, he dedicated his exhibition catalogue for the Moderne Galerie Bottrop to the painter, who was born in Bottrop.

62. Hilton Kramer, "Display of Judd Art Defines an Attitude," *The New York Times*, May 14, 1971, p. D48.

63. Judd, "Portfolio: 4 Sculptors," p. 44; *Complete Writings 1959–1975*, p. 196.

64. Loos went so far as to describe ornament as a crime; see his 1908 essay "Ornament and Crime," reprinted in Adolph Loos, *Trotzdem 1900–1930* (Vienna: Adolph Opel, 1982), pp. 78–88.

65. Hilton Kramer, "Primary Structures—The New Anonymity," *The New York Times*, May 1, 1966, p. D23; and Kramer, "An Art of Boredom?," *The New York Times*, June 5, 1966, p. D29.

66. John Perreault, "Union-Made Report on a Phenomenon," *Arts Magazine*, 61 (March 1967), pp. 26–31. Minimalism —which eventually prevailed as an epithet over Reductive Art, ABC Art, or Specific Objects—was less a specific stylistic designation than a container for a broadly based sensibility whose elasticity as a category is comparable to Cubism. As with Cubism, its fecundity seemed so great that it is now considered the sire of almost all of Post-Modernism—Conceptual, Body, and Process Art included. In this context, Judd's desire to separate himself from Minimalism is understandable. Moreover, although discourse about the Minimalist sensibility abounded, little effort was made to differentiate the artists. For example, Judd's work was invariably coupled with Robert Morris' memory-imprinting forms and even those who wrote perceptively on Judd's art often mistakenly ascribed to it the phenomenological goals and Gestalt readings that Morris propounded.

67. Clement Greenberg, "Recentness in Sculpture," in *American Sculpture of the Sixties,* exhibition catalogue, Los Angeles County Museum of Art, 1971, p. 25. For the attention generated by theoretical discourse, see Kramer, "An Art of Boredom?," p. D29.

68. Max Kozloff, "The Future Adventures of American Sculpture," *Arts Magazine,* 39 (February 1965), p. 26. Kozloff's verdict about this conceptual aspect was hardly positive: "these tenacious vacuities, manifestations of the sanitized, are also refuge for small spirits."

69. Barbara Rose, "ABC Art," *Art in America,* 53 (October–November 1965), pp. 69, 66.

70. Kramer, "Primary Structures—The New Anonymity," p. D23.

71. Judd, "Jackson Pollock," p. 34; *Complete Writings 1959–1975*, p. 195.

72. Perreault, "Union-Made Report on a Phenomenon," p. 30.

73. Judd sharply rejected a strict linear reading of art history: "The history of art and art's condition at any time are pretty messy," he wrote. "They should stay that way. . . . Styles, schools, common goals and long-term stability are

not credible ideas"; "Local History," p. 25; *Complete Writings 1959–1975*, pp. 150–151. For continuity in art, see Judd, "Milton Avery," *Arts Magazine*, 38 (December 1963), p. 61; *Complete Writings 1959–1975*, p. 106; and for this continuity as spatial illusionism, see Judd, "Local History," p. 22; *Complete Writings 1959–1975*, p. 150.

74. Judd, "Kenneth Noland," p. 54; *Complete Writings 1959–1975*, p. 93.

75. For "decisive advances," see Judd, "Frank Stella," *Arts Magazine*, 36 (September 1962), p. 51; *Complete Writings 1959–1975*, p. 57. Ibid. for Abstract Expressionism as an "inadequate style." For Abstract Expressionism as "old-fashioned" in its retention of spatial illusionism, see Judd, "Local History," p. 25; *Complete Writings 1959–1975*, p. 150.

76. Donald Kuspit, for example, saw Judd's recent writings as attempts to deny other people the right to an independent view on art; "Donald Judd," *Artforum*, 23 (February 1985), p. 92.

77. Like Greenberg, Judd rejected art that had subject matter. In this context, he identified the work of Rauschenberg and Johns as not "so momentous" and pejoratively characterized his life as having been lived in the shade of a coathanger and a bedspread; see "Complaints: Part I," *Studio International*, 177 (April 1969), p. 182; *Complete Writings 1959–1975*, p. 197, and Judd, "Two Contemporary Artists Comment," p. 250; *Complete Writings 1975–1986*, p. 17.

78. Lucy Lippard noted the death of painting in her essay "As Painting Is to Sculpture: A Change Ratio," in *American Sculpture of the Sixties*, p. 31.

79. Quoted in Rubin, *Frank Stella*, p. 70.

80. Greenberg, "Recentness in Sculpture," p. 24.

81. Michael Fried, "Art and Objecthood," *Artforum*, 5 (Summer 1967), p. 16.

82. Sanford Schwartz, "The Saatchi Collection, or a Generation Comes into Focus," *The New Criterion*, 4 (March 1986), p. 24.

83. "I've always thought that my work had political implications, had attitudes that would permit, limit or prohibit some kinds of political behavior and some institutions"; Donald Judd, "The Artist and Politics: A Symposium," *Artforum*, 8 (September 1970), p. 36, and "La Sfida del Sistema," *Metro*, no. 14 (June 1968), p. 43; *Complete Writings 1959–1975*, p. 196. "I object very much when my work is said to not be political because my feelings about the social system are in there somewhere"; "Interview with Donald Judd," *Flash Art*, no. 134 (May 1987), p. 36.

84. For a discussion of the relationship between non-hierarchical arrangement and politics, see Amy Goldin, "The Antihierarchical American," *Art News*, 66 (September 1967), pp. 48–52. Barbara Rose also equated Judd's non-relational composition with the non-stratified structure of American democracy in "Problems of Criticism, V," *Artforum*, 7 (January 1969), p. 45.

85. Judd, "La Sfida del Sistema," p. 43; *Complete Writings 1959–1975*, p. 196.

86. Donald Judd, "Imperialism, Nationalism and Regionalism," in *Complete Writings 1959–1975*, p. 222.

87. For Judd's disavowal of a connection between postwar art and postwar politics, see Jeff Perrone, "Seeing Through Boxes," *Artforum*, 15 (November 1976), p. 47.

88. Judd, "Imperialism, Nationalism and Regionalism," *Complete Writings 1959–1975*, p. 220.

89. Writing for the War Resisters League in 1968, Judd denounced American involvement in the Vietnam war and called for negotiations and a withdrawal of U.S. troops immediately; see "End the Killing in Vietnam," *The Aspen Times*, August 29, 1968, p. C21; *Complete Writings 1959–1975*, pp. 218–19. Judd was also an active member of his New York community and wrote a number of articles for the newspaper *Lower Manhattan Township*. In these, he demanded the preservation of the Cast Iron District of Manhattan and Soho and warned of the results of the development of those areas; *Complete Writings 1959–1975*, pp. 202–05. In 1975 Judd restated his political beliefs in relation to the arts in "Imperialism, Nationalism and Regionalism," *Complete Writings 1959–1975*, pp. 220–23.

90. See, for example, Suzi Gablik, "Don Judd: Drawings 1956–1976," *Studio International*, 193 (January 1977), p. 64. "The ontological and epistemological issues which [Judd's art] asserts, are very much under siege. . . . We seem to be passing from the lofty isolation of an art cut off from human purpose and intentions and therefore absolutely and timelessly valid."

91. Ibid., p. 64, and Gary Indiana, "Square Roots," The *Village Voice*, October 21, 1986, p. 84. To Lisa Liebmann, "Don Judd," *Artforum*, 20 (January 1982), p. 78, the secular hermeticism in Judd's sculpture bordered on the misanthropic.

92. Although Judd's style was ostensibly linked with the classical tradition, he rejected the term "classical" because, to him, it signified a relational type of composition epitomized in Poussin's paintings; Judd, "The Classical Spirit in Twentieth Century Art," *Arts Magazine*, 39 (April 1964), p. 28; *Complete Writings 1959–1975*, p. 123.

93. "Donald Judd: An Interview with John Coplans," p. 44.

94. Some stacks had less than ten units; one had fourteen.

95. One of Judd's multipart boxes that he allowed to be positioned on either the wall or floor was a sculpture consisting of four 40-inch galvanized boxes owned by Joseph Kosuth.

96. For a discussion of the hedonistic opulence of Judd's work, see Elizabeth Baker, "Judd the Obscure," *Art News*, 67 (April 1968), pp. 44–45, 60–64; and Kramer, "Display of Judd Art Defines an Attitude," p. D48.

97. Hilton Kramer, "Don Judd," *The New York Times*, February 9, 1979, p. C25.

98. For a discussion of seriality in twentieth century art, see John Coplans, *Serial Art*, exhibition catalogue, Pasadena Art Museum, 1968.

99. "Donald Judd," *The New York Times*, April 1, 1977, p. C20.

100. Kenneth Baker, "Donald Judd: Past Theory," *Artforum*, 15 (Summer 1977), p. 46.

101. For a discussion of this work, see Roberta Smith, "Multiple Returns," *Art in America*, 70 (March 1982), pp. 112–14.

102. Ibid., p. 114.

103. For the relationship between art and the unity that governs people's lives despite contradictory diversity, see Judd, "Yale Lecture," pp. 149–50.

104. For comparison of this work with a musical fugue, see Peter Schjeldahl, *Art in Our Time: The Saatchi Collection* (New York: Rizzoli, 1984), I, p. 18.

105. On March 14, 1964, Judd married Margaret Hughan Finch. Their first child, Flavin Starbuck, was born in 1968; their daughter, Rainer Yingling, was born two years later.

106. For description of vegetation, see Judd, "A Portrait of the Artist as His Own Man," p. 156; *Complete Writings 1975–1986*, p. 97.

107. Judd, "A Sense of Proportion," *Progressive Architecture*, 4 (April 1985) p. 104.

108. José Ortega y Gasset, quoted by Judd in "The Chinati Foundation," *The Chinati Foundation* (Marfa, Texas: The Chinati Foundation, 1987), unpaginated.

Donald Judd, 1986. Photograph by Robert Mapplethorpe.

Exhibition History

A bullet (•) indicates a one-artist exhibition. The listing of group exhibitions is selected.

1967

The Detroit Institute of Arts, Detroit. "Form-Color-Image." April–May.

Los Angeles County Museum of Art. "American Sculpture of the Sixties." April – June. Traveled to: Philadelphia Museum of Art.

The Washington Gallery of Modern Art, Washington, D.C. "A New Aesthetic." April–June.

The Saint Louis Art Museum. "7 for 67: Works by Contemporary American Sculptors." October–January.

The Solomon R. Guggenheim Museum, New York. "Guggenheim International Exhibition: Sculpture from 20 Nations." October 1967 – February 1968. Traveled to: Art Gallery of Ontario, Toronto; The National Gallery of Canada, Ottawa; Montreal Museum of Fine Arts.

Stedelijk Van Abbemuseum, Eindhoven, The Netherlands. "Kompass III." November–December.

1968

• Whitney Museum of American Art, New York. February–March.

Albright-Knox Art Gallery, Buffalo. "Plus by Minus." March–April.

Haags Gemeentemuseum, The Hague. "Minimal Art." March–May.

• Irving Blum Gallery, Los Angeles. May–June.

Kassel, West Germany. "Documenta 4." June –October.

The Museum of Modern Art, New York. "The Art of the Real: USA, 1948 – 1968." July – September.

1969

• Leo Castelli Gallery, New York. January.

Institute of Contemporary Art, University of Pennsylvania, Philadelphia. "Plastics and New Art." January–February.

The Museum of Modern Art, New York, organizer. "New Media: New Methods." Circulating exhibition, March 1969–April 1970.

• Galerie Ileana Sonnabend, Paris. May.

• Galerie Bischofsberger, Zurich. May–June.

Walker Art Center, Minneapolis. "Fourteen Sculptors: The Industrial Edge." May–June.

• Galerie Rudolph Zwirner, Cologne. June.

• Irving Blum Gallery, Los Angeles. September–November.

The Metropolitan Museum of Art, New York. "Painting and Sculpture: 1940–1970." October 1969–February 1970.

1970

• Stedelijk Van Abbemuseum, Eindhoven, The Netherlands. January–March.

The Art Institute of Chicago. "69th American Exhibition." January–February.

• The Helman Gallery, St. Louis. April.

• Leo Castelli Gallery and Warehouse, New York. April–May.

• Museum Folkwang, Essen, West Germany. April–May.

• Kunstverein Hannover, West Germany. June –August.

• Konrad Fischer, Düsseldorf. July.

• Locksley Shea Gallery, Minneapolis. September–October.

Contemporary Arts Center, Cincinnati. "Monumental Art." September–November.

San Francisco Museum of Modern Art. "Unitary Forms: Minimal Sculpture by Andre, Judd, McCracken and Smith." September–November.

1971

The Solomon R. Guggenheim Museum, New York. "The Guggenheim International Exhibition 1971." February–April.

• Pasadena Art Museum. May–July.

Walker Art Center, Minneapolis. "Work for New Spaces." May–July.

Park Sonsbeek, Arnhem, The Netherlands. "Sonsbeek Buiten de Perken." June–August.

Louisiana Museum of Modern Art, Humlebaek, Denmark. "Amerikansk Kunst." September–October.

1972

Leo Castelli Gallery, New York. "Serra-Judd." May–June.

• Greenberg Gallery, St. Louis. November–December.

• Galerie Rolf Ricke, Cologne. November–December.

• Galerie Daniel Templon, Paris. December 1972–January 1973.

1973

• Leo Castelli Gallery, New York. January–February.

• Galleria Gian Enzo Sperone and Konrad Fischer, Rome. March.

• Locksley Shea Gallery, Minneapolis. April.

Seattle Art Museum Pavilion. "American Art: Third Quarter Century." August–October.

• Galleria Gian Enzo Sperone, Turin. September–November.

1974

• Lisson Gallery, London. January–February.

Art Museum of South Texas, Corpus Christi. "Eight Artists: Christensen, Jenney, Judd, Lichtenstein, Rauschenberg, Stephan, Twombly, Young." February–March. Traveled to: Miami Art Center.

National Gallery of Victoria, Melbourne, organized by The Museum of Modern Art, New York. "Some Recent American Art." February–March. Traveled to: Art Gallery of New South Wales, Sydney; Art Gallery of South Australia, Adelaide; The Art Gallery of Western Australia, Perth; City of Auckland Art Gallery, Auckland.

• Ace Gallery, Venice, California. April–May.

John F. Kennedy Center for the Performing Arts, Washington, D.C. "Art Now." May–June.

• Portland Center for the Visual Arts. November–December.

1975

Rijksmuseum Kröller-Müller, Otterlo, The Netherlands. "Functions of Drawing." May – June.

- The National Gallery of Canada, Ottawa. May – July.
- Galerie Daniel Templon, Paris. June – July.
- Lisson Gallery, London. September – October.

National Collection of Fine Arts, Smithsonian Institution, Washington, D.C. "Sculpture: American Directions 1945 – 1975." October – November.

1976

Whitney Museum of American Art, New York. "200 Years of American Sculpture." March – September.

- Leo Castelli Gallery, New York. March – April.
- Kunsthalle Bern, Switzerland. April – May.
- Kunstmuseum Basel, Switzerland. April – June. Traveled to: Kunsthalle Tübingen; Museum Moderner Kunst / Museum des 20. Jahrhunderts, Vienna; Musée d'Art et d'Histoire, Geneva.
- Janie C. Lee Gallery, Houston. October – November.
- Sable-Castelli Gallery, Toronto. October.
- Museum of Modern Art, Oxford. November – December.

1977

- Art Museum of South Texas, Corpus Christi. January – March.
- Heiner Friedrich, New York. March – April.
- Heiner Friedrich, Cologne. May – June.
- Moderne Galerie Bottrop, Bottrop, West Germany. May – June.
- Contemporary Arts Center, Cincinnati. June – July.
- Ace Gallery, Venice, California. August – September.

The New York State Museum, Albany. "New York: The State of Art." October – November.

1978

- Nationalgalerie, Berlin. January.
- Leo Castelli Gallery, New York. March.
- Rijksmuseum Kröller-Müller, Otterlo, The Netherlands. March – May.
- Foyer MGB, Zurich. April.
- Vancouver Art Gallery, Vancouver. May – June.
- Heiner Friedrich, Munich. May – June.
- Heiner Friedrich, New York. September – October.
- Young-Hoffman Gallery, Chicago. October.

1979

- Leo Castelli Gallery, New York. February.

Institute of Contemporary Art, Boston. "The Reductive Object: A Survey of the Minimalist Aesthetic in the 1960's." March – April.

- Stedelijk Van Abbemuseum, Eindhoven, The Netherlands. April.
- Lisson Gallery, London. May – June.
- Akron Art Institute, Ohio. May – June.
- Heiner Friedrich, Cologne. June – November.

Milwaukee Art Museum. "Emergence & Progression: Six Contemporary American Artists." October – December. Traveled to: Virginia Museum of Fine Arts, Richmond; J.B. Speed Art Museum, Louisville; New Orleans Museum of Art.

- Thomas Segal Gallery, Boston. November.
- Galerie Annemarie Verna, Zurich. November 1979 – January 1980.

1980

Kunstmuseum Düsseldorf. "Sammlung Panza: Minimal Skulpturen." September – November.

1981

Museen der Stadt Köln, Cologne. "Westkunst: Zeitgenössische Kunst seit 1939." May – August.

- Leo Castelli Gallery, New York. September – October.
- Newport Harbor Art Museum, Newport Beach, California. September – November.

1982

Kunstmuseum Basel. "Johns/Judd/LeWitt/ Neuman/ Stella." January.

- Larry Gagosian Gallery, Los Angeles. May – June.

Kassel. "Documenta 7." June – September.

1983

Tyler Museum of Art, Texas. "Concepts in Construction: 1910 – 1980." February – March. Traveled to: R.W. Norton Gallery, West Palm Beach, Florida; Bass Museum of Art, Miami Beach; Cincinnati Art Museum; Alberta College of Art, Calgary; Norman Mackenzie Art Gallery, University of Regina, Saskatchewan; Anchorage Museum of History and Art, Alaska; Long Beach Museum of Art, California; Palm Springs Desert Museum, California; Neuberger Museum, State University of New York, College at Purchase.

- Leo Castelli Gallery, New York. April – June.
- Carol Taylor Art, Dallas. October.

Kunstmuseum Athenaeum, Helsinki. "Art 83 Helsinki." October – December.

Museum of Contemporary Art, Los Angeles. "Opening Show." November 1983 – February 1964.

- Knight Gallery, "Eight Works in Three Dimensions." Charlotte, North Carolina. November 1983 – January 1984.
- Blum Helman Gallery, New York. November – December.

1984

- Neuberger Museum, State University of New York, College at Purchase. March – July.

Merian-Park, Basel, Switzerland. "Skulptur im 20. Jahrhundert." June – September.

Whitney Museum of American Art, New York. "Blam! The Explosion of Pop, Minimalism, and Performance." September–December.

- Margo Leavin Gallery, Los Angeles. October–November.

- Leo Castelli Gallery, New York. November–December.

- Max Protetch Gallery, New York. December.

1985

- Galerie Annemarie Verna, Zurich. February–April.

Art Center College of Design, Pasadena. "Furniture Design by Donald Judd/Robert Venturi." March–April.

- Galleria Lia Rumma, Naples. March–April.

- Texas Gallery, Houston. May–June.

- Galerie Bärbel Grässlin, Frankfurt. September–October.

Whitney Museum of American Art, New York. "High Styles: Twentieth-Century American Design." September 1985–February 1986.

- Rhona Hoffman Gallery, Chicago. October–November.

The Solomon R. Guggenheim Museum, New York. "Transformation in Sculpture." November 1985–February 1986.

Frankfurter Kunstverein, Frankfurt. "Vom Zeichnen: Aspekte der Zeichnung 1960–1985." November 1985–January 1986. Traveled to: Kasseler Kunstverein, Kassel, West Germany; Museum Moderner Kunst, Vienna.

1986

- Waddington Galleries, London. March.

Museum Haus Lange, Krefeld, West Germany. "Beuys, Judd, Oldenburg und Serra." March–April.

École Regionale des Beaux-Arts Georges Pompidou, Dunkerque, France. "Minimal et Conceptuel." April–May.

David Winton Bell Gallery, List Art Center, Brown University, Providence, Rhode Island.

"Definitive Statements: American Art 1964–66." May–June. Traveled to: The Parrish Art Museum, Southampton, New York.

Galerie Aronowitsch, Stockholm. "En Subjektiv Historia." September.

- Paula Cooper Gallery, New York. October–November.

The Museum of Contemporary Art, Los Angeles. "Individuals: A Selected History of Contemporary Art 1945–1986." December 1986–January 1988.

1987

- Galerie Rolf Ricke, Cologne. February–March.

- Margo Leavin Gallery, Los Angeles. February–March.

Westfälisches Landesmuseum, Münster, West Germany. "Skulptur Projekte in Münster." March–April. Traveled to: Städtisches Museum Abteiberg, Mönchengladbach, West Germany.

Institute of Contemporary Art, University of Pennsylvania, Philadelphia. "1967: At the Crossroads." March–April.

- Galerie Maeght Lelong, Paris. April–May.

- Stedelijk Van Abbemuseum, Eindhoven, The Netherlands. April–June. Traveled to: Städtische Kunsthalle Düsseldorf; Musée d'Art Moderne de la Ville de Paris; Fundació Joan Miró, Barcelona.

Musée National d'Art Moderne, Centre Georges Pompidou, Paris. "L'Epoque, la Mode, la Morale, la Passion: Aspects de l'Art d'Aujourd'hui 1977–1987." May–August.

Centro Cultural Arte Contemporaneo, Mexico City. "Leo Castelli y Sus Artistas." June–October.

Butler Institute of American Art, Youngstown, Ohio. "Leo Castelli: A Tribute Exhibition." June–September.

- Galerie Annemarie Verna, Zurich. November 1987–January 1988.

1988

- Lawrence Oliver Gallery, Philadelphia. March–April.

- Galerie Nachst St. Stephan, Vienna. March–April.

- Galerie Aronowitsch, Stockholm. March–April.

Selected Bibliography

Bibliographical material is listed alphabetically by author or, in the case of exhibition catalogues, by institution.

Agee, William C. "Unit, Series, Site: A Judd Lexicon." *Art in America*, 63 (May–June 1975), pp. 40–49.

Baker, Elizabeth C. "Judd the Obscure." *Art News*, 67 (April 1968), pp. 44–45, 60–63.

Baker, Kenneth. "Donald Judd: Past Theory." *Artforum*, 15 (Summer 1977), pp. 46–47.

Battcock, Gregory, ed. *Minimal Art: A Critical Anthology*. New York: E.P. Dutton, 1968.

Bickers, Patricia. "Scaled-down Judd: Donald Judd at Waddington's." *Art Monthly*, 95 (April 1986), pp. 20–22.

Burnett, David. "Donald Judd: The National Gallery of Canada." *ArtsCanada*, 32 (Winter 1975–76), pp. 28–32.

Carlson, Prudence. "Donald Judd's Equivocal Objects." *Art in America*, 72 (January 1984), pp. 114–18.

David Winton Bell Gallery, List Art Center, Brown University, Providence, Rhode Island. *Definitive Statements: American Art 1964–1966*. Exhibition catalogue, with texts by Michael Plante, Christopher Campbell, Megan Fox, Mitchell F. Merling, Jennifer Wells, and Ima Ebong, 1986.

Ennis, Michael. "The Marfa Art War." *Texas Monthly*, 12 (August 1984), pp. 138–42, 186–92.

Fried, Michael. "Art and Objecthood." *Artforum*, 5 (Summer 1967), pp. 12–23.

Friedman, Martin. "The Nart-Art of Donald Judd." *Art and Artists*, 1 (February 1967), pp. 58–61.

Gold, Barbara. "Artist Seeks Validity in Boxes." *The Baltimore Sunday Sun*, March 3, 1968, pp. D1–3.

Goldin, Amy. "The Antihierarchical American." *Art News*, 66 (September 1967), pp. 48–50, 64–65.

Institute of Contemporary Art, University of Pennsylvania, Philadelphia. *7 Sculptors*. Exhibition catalogue, with text by Robert Smithson, 1965.

The Jewish Museum, New York. *Primary Structures: Younger American and British Sculptors*. Exhibition catalogue, with text by Kynaston McShine, 1966.

Knight Gallery, Charlotte, North Carolina. *Eight Works in Three Dimensions*. Exhibition catalogue, with texts by Brian Wallis and Donald Judd, 1983.

Kramer, Hilton. "Art: An Art of Boredom?" *The New York Times*, June 5, 1966, p. D23.

Krauss, Rosalind. "Allusion and Illusion in Donald Judd." *Artforum*, 4 (May 1966), pp. 24–26.

_____. *Passages in Modern Sculpture*. New York: The Viking Press, 1977, chap. 7.

_____. "Sculpture in the Expanded Field." *October*, 8 (Spring 1979), pp. 31–44.

_____. "Sense and Sensibility: Reflection on Post '60s Sculpture." *Artforum*, 12 (November 1973), pp. 43–53.

Kunsthalle Bern, Switzerland. *Donald Judd: Skulpturen*. Exhibition catalogue, with texts by Johannes Gachnang and Donald Judd, 1976.

Kunstmuseum Basel, Switzerland. *Donald Judd: Zeichnungen/Drawings 1956–1976*. Exhibition catalogue, with text by Dieter Koepplin, 1976.

Leider, Philip. "Literalism and Abstraction: Frank Stella's Retrospective at the Modern." *Artforum*, 8 (April 1970), pp. 44–47.

Lippard, Lucy R. "The Third Stream: Constructed Paintings and Painted Structures." *Art Voices*, 4 (Spring 1965), pp. 44–50.

Los Angeles County Museum of Art. *American Sculpture of the Sixties*. Exhibition catalogue edited by Maurice Tuchman, with texts by Lawrence Alloway, Wayne V. Andersen, Dore Ashton, John Coplans, Clement Greenberg, Max Kozloff, Lucy R. Lippard, James Monte, Barbara Rose, Irving Sandler, 1967.

Louw, Roelof. "Judd and After." *Studio International*, 184 (November 1972), pp. 171–75.

Mellow, James R. "Everything Sculpture Has My Work Doesn't." *The New York Times,* March 10, 1968, p. D21.

Millet, Catherine. "La Petite Logique de Donald Judd." *Art Press,* no. 119 (November 1987), pp. 4–10.

Milwaukee Art Museum. *Emergence & Progression: Six Contemporary American Artists.* Exhibition catalogue, with text by I. Michael Danoff, 1979.

Moderne Galerie Bottrop, Bottrop, West Germany. *Donald Judd.* Exhibition catalogue, with interview by Kasper König, 1977.

Muller, Gregoire. "Donald Judd: Ten Years." *Arts Magazine,* 47 (February 1973), pp. 35–42.

The Museum of Contemporary Art, Los Angeles. *Individuals: A Selected History of Contemporary Art 1945–1986.* Exhibition catalogue, with text on Minimalism by Hal Foster, 1986.

National Gallery of Canada, Ottawa. *Donald Judd: Catalogue Raisonné of Paintings, Objects, and Wood-Blocks 1960–1974.* Exhibition catalogue, with texts by Jean Sutherland Boggs, Brydon Smith, Dan Flavin, and Roberta Smith, 1975.

Perreault, John. "A Minimal Future? Union-Made: Report on a Phenomenon." *Arts Magazine,* 41 (March 1967), pp. 26–31.

Perrone, Jeff. "Seeing Through the Boxes." *Artforum,* 15 (November 1976), pp. 45–47.

Pincus-Witten, Robert. "Fining It Down: Don Judd at Castelli." *Artforum,* 8 (June 1970), pp. 47–49.

Reise, Barbara. "'Untitled 1969': A Footnote on Art and Minimal Stylehood." *Studio International,* 177 (April 1969), pp. 165–72.

Rose, Barbara. "ABC Art." *Art in America,* 53 (October–November 1965), pp. 57–69.

———. "Donald Judd." *Artforum,* 3 (June 1965), pp. 30–32.

———. "Problems of Criticism V: The Politics of Art, Part II." *Artforum* 7 (January 1969), pp. 44–49.

Schjeldahl, Peter. *Art of Our Times: The Saatchi Collection,* Volume 1. New York: Rizzoli, 1984.

Smith, Roberta. "Multiple Returns." *Art in America,* 70 (March 1982), pp. 112–14.

———. "Two Critics Collected." *Art in America,* 64 (November – December 1976), pp. 35–37.

Stedelijk Van Abbemuseum, Eindhoven, The Netherlands. *Donald Judd.* Exhibition catalogue, with texts by R. H. Fuchs and Rainer Crone, 1987.

Stein, William F. "Donald Judd: The Project at Marfa." *Cite: The Architecture and Design Review of Houston* (Spring–Summer 1988), pp. 9–12.

Vancouver Art Gallery. *Donald Judd.* Exhibition catalogue, with texts by Luke Rombout, Brydon Smith, and Donald Judd, 1978.

Walker Art Center, Minneapolis. *14 Sculptors: The Industrial Edge.* Exhibition catalogue, with texts by Martin Friedman, Barabara Rose, and Christopher Finch, 1969.

The Washington Gallery of Modern Art, Washington, D.C. *A New Aesthetic.* Exhibition catalogue, with text by Barbara Rose, 1967.

Whitney Museum of American Art, New York. *Don Judd.* Exhibition catalogue, with texts by William C. Agee, Dan Flavin, and Donald Judd, 1968.

Artist's Writings and Interviews

Donald Judd's writings have been compiled in the following two volumes:

Judd, Donald. *Complete Writings 1959–1975: Gallery Reviews, Book Reviews, Articles, Letters to the Editor, Reports, Statements, Complaints.* Halifax: The Press of the Nova Scotia College of Art and Design; New York: New York University Press, 1975.

———. *Complete Writings 1975–1986.* Eindhoven, The Netherlands: Stedelijk Van Abbemuseum, 1987.

Additional statements and interviews:

Glaser, Bruce. "Questions to Stella and Judd." *Art News,* 65 (September 1966), pp. 55–61.

Galerie Sonnabend, Paris. *Don Judd: Structures.* Exhibition catalogue, with text by Donald Judd, 1969.

Statement in "The Artist and Politics: A Symposium," *Artforum,* 9 (September 1970), pp. 35–39.

Kunstverein Hannover, West Germany. *Don Judd.* Exhibition catalogue, with texts by Manfred de la Motte, Donald Judd, Martin Friedman, Philip Leider, and Bruce Glaser, 1970.

Pasadena Art Museum. *Don Judd.* Exhibition catalogue, with text and interview by John Coplans, 1971.

Siegel, Jeanne. "Around Barnett Newman: Interviews with and Statements by Twelve Painters and Sculptors." *Art News,* 70 (October 1971), pp. 42–47, 59–65.

Moderne Galerie Bottrop, Bottrop, West Germany. *Donald Judd.* Exhibition catalogue, with interview by Kasper König, 1977.

"A Sense of Proportion." *Progressive Architecture,* 4 (April 1985), pp. 102–09. Text by Donald Judd with introduction by Pilar Viladas.

Galerie Maeght Lelong, Paris. *Judd.* Exhibition catalogue, with text by Donald Judd, 1987.

Taylor, Paul. "Interview with Donald Judd." *Flash Art,* 134 (May 1987), pp. 35–37.

Works in the Exhibition

Dimensions are in inches, followed by centimeters; height precedes width precedes depth.

Untitled, 1961
Oil and Liquitex on canvas, 50⅞ x 111⅜ (129.2 x 282.9)
Collection of the artist

Untitled, 1962
Oil and wax on canvas, 69 x 101¾ (175.3 x 258.5)
Collection of the artist

Untitled, 1962
Cadmium red light oil on wood with black enameled metal pipe, 48 x 33⅛ x 21¾ (122 x 84 x 54.6)
Kunstmuseum Basel

Untitled, 1962
Cadmium red light oil and wax on Liquitex, sand on masonite and wood, and aluminum and black oil on wood, 48 x 96 x 7½ (122 x 243.8 x 19)
Collection of the artist

Untitled, 1962
Cadmium red light oil and wax on Liquitex and sand on masonite with yellow plexiglass, 48 x 96 x 2½ (122 x 243.8 x 6.4)
Collection of Gerald S. Elliott

Untitled, 1963
Cadmium red light oil on wood, 19½ x 45 x 30½ (49.5 x 114.3 x 77.5)
Collection of Gordon Locksley and George T. Shea

Untitled, 1963
Cadmium red light and black oil on wood with galvanized iron and aluminum, 76 x 96 x 11¾ (193 x 243.8 x29.8)
Collection of Robert A.M. Stern

Untitled, 1963
Black enamel on aluminum, raw sienna enamel, and galvanized iron on wood, 52 x 42⅛ x 5⅞ (132 x 107 x 15)
Collection of Gerald S. Elliott

Untitled, 1963 (reconstructed in 1988)
Cadmium red light oil on wood with violet plexiglass, 20 x 48⅝ x 47⅝ (50.8 x 123.5 x 121)
Collection of the artist; Courtesy Chinati Foundation, Marfa, Texas

Untitled, 1963 (reconstructed in 1988)
Cadmium red light oil on wood and purple enamel on aluminum, 48 x 83 x 48 (122 x 210.8 x 122)
Collection of the artist; Courtesy Chinati Foundation, Marfa, Texas

Untitled, 1963
Cadmium red light oil on wood with metal lathe, 72 x 104 x 49 (182.9 x 264.2 x 124.5)
Collection of the artist; Courtesy Chinati Foundation, Marfa, Texas

Untitled, 1964
Chartreuse oil on wood and yellow enamel on iron, 19½ x 48 x 34 (49.5 x 122 x 86.4)
Helman Collection, New York

Untitled, 1965
Perforated 16-gauge cold-rolled steel, 8 x 120 x 66 (20.3 x 304.8 x 167.6)
Whitney Museum of American Art, New York; 50th Anniversary Gift of Toiny and Leo Castelli   79.77

Untitled, 1965
Red lacquer on galvanized iron, 14½ x 76½ x 25½ (36.8 x 194.3 x 64.8)
Walker Art Center, Minneapolis; Harold D. Field Memorial Acquisition

Untitled, 1966
Turquoise enamel on cold-rolled steel, ten units: 48 x 120 x 6⅝ (122 x 304.8 x 16.8) each, with 6 in. (15.2 cm) intervals
Whitney Museum of American Art, New York; Gift of Howard and Jean Lipman   72.7

Untitled, 1967
Galvanized iron with green lacquer on front and sides, twelve units: 9 x 40 x 31 (23 x 101.6 x 78.7) each, with 9 in. (23 cm) intervals
Helman Collection, New York

Untitled, 1968
Stainless steel and amber plexiglass, six units: 34 x 34 x 34 (86.4 x 86.4 x 86.4) each, with 8 in. (20.3 cm) intervals
Milwaukee Art Museum; Layton Art Collection

Untitled, 1968
Stainless steel and plexiglass, 33 x 68 x 48 (83.8 x 172.7 x 122)
Whitney Museum of American Art, New York; Purchase, with funds from the Howard and Jean Lipman Foundation, Inc.   68.36

Untitled, 1969
Brass and red fluorescent plexiglass, ten units: 6⅛ x 24 x 27 (15.2 x 68.6 x 62) each, with 6 in. (15.2 cm) intervals
Hirshhorn Museum and Sculpture Garden, Smithsonian Institution, Washington, D.C.; Gift of Joseph H. Hirshhorn

Untitled, 1969
Clear anodized aluminum and blue plexiglass, four units: 48 x 60 x 60 (122 x 152.4 x 152.4) each, with 12 in. (30.4 cm) intervals
The Saint Louis Art Museum; Gift of the Schoenberg Foundation

Untitled, 1970
Gray-amber plexiglass and stainless steel, 20 x 48 x 34 (50.8 x 122 x 86.4)
Collection of Gordon Locksley and George T. Shea

Untitled, 1970
Hot-dipped galvanized iron, thirteen of eighteen units: 12 units, 60 x 48 (152.4 x 122) each; 1 unit, 60 x 13 (152.4 x 33)
Collection of the artist

Untitled, 1971
Blue anodized aluminum, six units: 48 x 48 x 48 (122 x 122 x 122) each
Walker Art Center, Minneapolis; Gift of the T.B. Walker Foundation

Untitled, 1972
Clear anodized aluminum and galvanized iron, 8¼ x 161 x 8 (21 x 409 x 20.3)
Collection of Bernar Venet

Untitled, 1972
Chartreuse anodized aluminum, 14½ x 76½ x 25½ (36.8 x 194.3 x 64.8)
Collection of the artist

Untitled, 1974
Blue lacquer on aluminum and fluorescent orange resin on wood, 16½ x 69 x 5 (41.9 x 175.3 x 12.7)
Collection of Gordon Locksley and George T. Shea, Locksley/Shea Gallery

Untitled, 1975
Brass and chartreuse anodized aluminum, 6 x 110¾ x 6 (15.2 x 281.3 x 15.2)
Collection of Mr. and Mrs. J. Gary Gradinger

Untitled, 1975
Brass and red enamel on aluminum, 36⅛ x 60 x 60 (91.8 x 152.4 x 152.4)
The Museum of Fine Arts, Houston; Museum purchase with funds provided by the National Endowment for the Arts and matched by the Brown Foundation

Untitled, 1979
Copper and red anodized aluminum, 5¼ x 75¾ x 5 (13.3 x 192.4 x 12.7)
Margo Leavin Gallery, Los Angeles

Untitled, 1982
Aluminum and violet plexiglass, three units: 39⅜ x 39⅜ x 12½ (100 x 100 x 32) each
Collection of Annemarie and Gianfranco Verna

Untitled, 1982
Brass and anodized aluminum, 40½ x 84 x 6¾ (102.8 x 213.4 x 17.1)
The Dayton Art Institute, Ohio; Museum purchase with funds provided by NCR Corporation

Untitled, 1984
Painted aluminum, 11¾ x 71 x 11¾ (30 x 180 x 30)
Collection of Marcia S. Weisman

Untitled, 1984
Painted aluminum, 11¾ x 71 x 11¾ (30 x 180 x 30)
Collection of Douglas S. Cramer

Untitled, 1984
Aluminum with blue plexiglass over black plexiglass, six units: 19¹¹⁄₁₆ x 39⅜ x 19¹¹⁄₁₆ (50 x 100 x 50) each, with 12 in. (30.5 cm) intervals
Whitney Museum of American Art, New York; Purchase, with funds from the Brown Foundation, Inc. in memory of Margaret Root Brown   85.14a–f

Untitled, 1984
Corten steel and purple plexiglass, two units: 39⅜ x 39⅜ x 19¹¹⁄₁₆ (100 x 100 x 50) each, with 19¹¹⁄₁₆ in. (50 cm) intervals
Collection of Asher B. Edelman

Untitled, 1984
Copper and clear plexiglass, ten units: 6 x 27 x 24 (15.2 x 68.6 x 61) each, with 6 in. (15.2 cm) intervals
Collection of Mr. and Mrs. Samuel Heyman

Untitled, 1986–88 (in progress)
Plywood and colored plexiglass, thirty-three units: 39⅜ x 39⅜ x 19¹¹⁄₁₆ (100 x 100 x 50) each
Collection of the artist

Untitled, 1988
Galvanized iron, four units: 40 x 40 x 40 (101.6 x 101.6 x 101.6) each
Collection of the artist

Untitled, 1988
Concrete, four units: 98⁷⁄₁₆ x 98⁷⁄₁₆ x 98⁷⁄₁₆ (250 x 250 x 250) each
Collection of the artist

Untitled, 1988
Painted aluminum, 30 x 240 x 30 (76.2 x 609.6 x 76.2)
Collection of the artist

Untitled, 1988
Turquoise pebbled plexiglass and stainless steel, 20 x 48 x 34 (50.8 x 122 x 86.4)
Collection of the artist

Untitled, 1988
Aluminum with yellow plexiglass, six units: 19¹¹⁄₁₆ x 39⅜ x 19¹¹⁄₁₆ (50 x 100 x 50) each
Collection of the artist; Courtesy Paula Cooper Gallery, New York

Untitled, 1988
Corten steel, 39⅜ x 78¾ x 78¾ (100 x 200 x 200)
Collection of the artist

Untitled, 1988
Clear anodized aluminum and amber plexiglass, two units: 19¹¹⁄₁₆ x 39⅜ x 19¹¹⁄₁₆ (50 x 100 x 50) each
Collection of the artist

Untitled, 1988
Concrete, 19¹¹⁄₁₆ x 19¹¹⁄₁₆ x 39⅜ (50 x 50 x 100)
Collection of the artist

This publication was organized at the Whitney Museum of American Art by Doris Palca, Head, Publications and Sales; Sheila Schwartz, Editor; Marsha Selikoff, Associate Editor; Vicki Drake, Supervisor, Printing Services; and Mary DelMonico, Secretary/Assistant.

It was designed by Anita Meyer, Boston, typeset in Helvetica by Monotype Composition, Boston, and printed on Vintage Velvet by Franklin Graphics, Rhode Island.